INTRODUCTION TO DATA ORGANISATION AND MANAGEMENT

DATA, INFORMATION AND KNOWLEDGE MANAGEMENT

Table of Contents	
2.1	Introduction
2.2	Objectives
2.3	Data organization
2.4	Data management
2.5	Information management
2.6	Knowledge management
2.7	the data life-cycle
2.8	Data, information and knowledge management compared
2.9	Summary
2.10	Self-assessment exercises
2.11	

2.1 Introduction

In this unit you will learn about the purposes of data organization and management, as well as those of information and knowledge management. You will also learn about the different data management activities that may be performed during the data life-cycle. Your earlier understanding of the relationships between data, information and knowledge will help you to understand why data management is usually associated with information and knowledge systems. It will also help you to understand how data management supports information management within information systems.

2.2 Objectives

After studying this unit, you should be able to:

1. Explain the purposes of data management.
2. Describe data management activities in the context of the data life cycle.
3. Explain the relationship between data management, information management and knowledge management.

2.3 Data organization

Data organization is concerned with the selection, combination, arrangement and formatting of symbols such as words, numbers and images to form data. The aim of data organization is to facilitate effective storage, transfer, computation or interpretation of the data by either human beings or machines.

You will recall from unit 1 that data are invariably created to express or convey information. However, data can be created out of different combinations of symbols including words, numbers, graphs, pictures, sound, etc. data organizations entail the analysis and applications of strategies for selecting, combining and using words, numbers and other types of symbols to create data for expressing information.

Data organization as a subject of study focuses on the analysis and application of appropriate methods, procedures and techniques for determining, for instance, how:

(a) Words, sentences and paragraphs are, or should be selected, written and arranged by an author into chapters of a textbook for, say, 100- level students;

(b) Statistical data are, or should be, arranged into informative tables;

(c) Menu items, icons, tool bars, words, etc. are, or should be, displayed in the windows of a computer screen;

(d) News items and other stories are, or should be, arranged in a newspaper edition;

(e) Data of different types should be defined and organized for efficient storage and retrieval in a computer;

(f) Data on the books held by a library are, or should be, written as catalogue entries to facilitate effective user access to the books;

(g) Entries in a back-of-book index are, or should be, arranged;

(h) How the questions in a survey questionnaire or application form are, or should be, arranged;

(1) The data to be included in resume should be arranged;

(i) (j) The names of the NOUN students offering 'Introduction to Data Organization and Management' should be arranged in a particular new list; etc.

(j) In this course you will learn about general and specific principles of organization in some of the contexts listed above. By grasping these principles, you will be equipped not only to quickly recognize problems of data organization that may arise in your personal life, professional career and work place, but also how to solve them through the application of the principles that you had learnt.

Exercise 2.1

Study carefully Chapter I of any textbook of your choice, and explain what you observe in terms of the arrangement, formatting, and organization of the content of the chapter.

Hint: How have the author and publisher arranged such things as the titles, subsection headings, etc? How are paragraphs separated from one another? Where is the page number shown? What numbering methods are used for lists of items? How much white margins are provided? What character sizes (large small. tiny, etc) and typefaces (bold, italics, underlining, etc) are used for different things? Guess why the author and publisher adopted those techniques and styles for arranging, formatting and organizing the data on the page.

2.4 Data management

Data management refers to the various activities that must be performed by individuals or organizations to ensure that only useful data are created for conveying information; that the data are appropriately organized, analyzed, stored and retrieved; that data are efficiently transferred across space and time as needed; that data are effectively protected from loss or damage; and that data are properly interpreted, analyzed and used to obtain information. Clearly, data organization is an aspect of data management.

2.5 The data management cycle

A useful approach to explaining data management activities is to consider the series of processes that may be undertaken over time in respect of data. The series of processes is collectively referred to as the data (or information) life- cycle. The data life-cycle traces the different data management activities that may be performed on data. Data management processes in the life-cycle are shown in Figure 2.1.

They are:

(i) Data policy making
(ii) Data definition and structuring
(iii) Data collection and creation
(vi) Data validation and quality control
(vi) Data analysis and summarization
(v) Data storage and retrieval
(ix) Data archiving and protection
(vii) Data communication and transfer
(viii) Data display and presentation

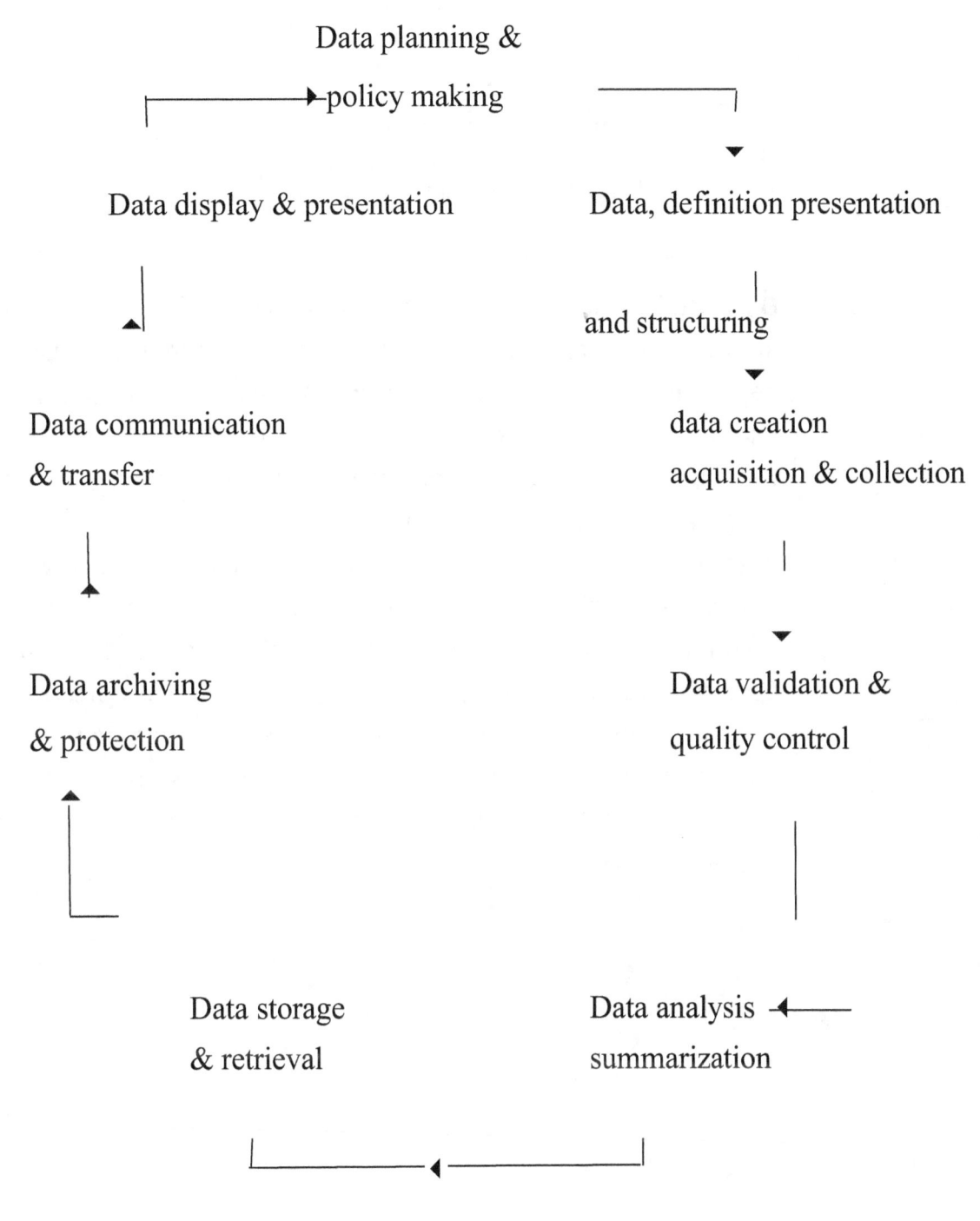

Figure 2.1

The data (information) life-cycle of activities

I will now briefly explain each of the stages.

2.8.1 **Data policy-making:** refers to the process of making decisions about what data should be created and for what purpose. Such decisions are very important in that they determine the ultimate usefulness and value of the data, as well as the cost of managing the data. For instance, before collecting data in a research study, a researcher must determine why he must collect data, what data to collect, as well as how, where, when and from whom to collect the data. In other words, data policy making entails planning what data to create, collect, store, analyze and transfer. Careful data planning and policy- making is important in all contexts, but more so in situations where the various data management activities are likely to consume substantial resources, or where data management mistakes can be very costly.

2.8.2 Data definition and structuring refers to the process of determining the formats in which data will be created, acquired, stored and transferred. This often requires specifying in detail what types of words, numbers; graphical images and sounds will be created, collected, acquired and stored. This entails, deciding for instance whether temperature will be measured in degree Fahrenheit or Celsius, and to how many decimal places; whether names of people will be recorded in the order of surname, first name, and middle name, or in some other order; whether photographs of people taken in colour or in just black and white, and so on.

2.8.3 Data collection and creation refers to the process of actually creating or collecting data in line with the data policies in (i) above, and the defined data definitions in (ii) above. This may entail

Composing combinations of symbols to create new data;

Using mechanical equipment (e.g. A weight scale) to measure variables, and then recording the measured values;

Using computer devices to capture data automatically as events take place;

Copying existing data from various data and information sources such as books, journals, statistical publications, computers, etc.

Representing with data the opinions expressed by people on a questionnaire, or in interviews;

Data collection may be undertaken in a variety of contexts: in a laboratory, as homes, during a national census; in educational institutions, as students register for different programmes and courses.

2.8.4 **Data validation and quality control** refers to the process of verifying and certifying that the data that have been created, collected or acquired from other sources meet certain minimum standards of accuracy and consistency. Both human and automated methods can be used for data validation and quality control. An example of a human system is to require a supervisor to cross-check the data that typists had typed or that customer had written on forms. An example of a computer-based approach is to use special computer software to check the spelling of the words in a computer document.

2.8.5 **Data analysis and summarization** refers to the different processes for comparing and analyzing data, and for computing, aggregating and summarizing data into other data such as statistics, charts, maps, abstracts and summaries. Different types of strategies are used for data analysis and summarization. For instance, statisticians use formula to analyse different types of data. And information scientists analyze, and compose abstracts of the data in different types of documents.

2.8.6 **Data storage and retrieval** refers to the physical storage and retrieval of data from different types of media, such as paper and computer media. Paper has been the traditional medium for storing and retrieving data and information. However, data storage and retrieval is now increasingly performed in databases created on computer media such as disks and tapes. Data often need to be reformatted or re-structured to ensure that they can be efficiently stored on, and quickly retrieved from, such media. Special computer software known as database management systems are used to create and manage the databases. The fundamental principle about data storage and retrieval is that data should always be stored carefully and systematically to enable fast and efficient retrieval of the data at a later time.

2.8.7 **Data archiving and protection** refers to the process of providing either special protection or secure long-term storage for extremely valuable data. Data protection are often performed to ensure that data are protected from loss, theft or damage, and guarded from people who should not have access to the data. Data may also be archived in media and storage spaces that can withstand environmental hazards such as temperature, humidity, fire, flood, etc. For example, the transactional data of a commercial bank are very valuable for obvious reasons; hence special data protection measures will be put in place by the bank to ensure that the data are not destroyed, stolen or tampered with. The bank will usually also make copies of such valuable data for storage in secure locations so that it would be able to replace the data in case of a disaster to the original data.

2.8.8 **Data communication and transfer** refers to the process of transporting data across space and time through different media such as documents and computer and telephone networks. Actually, data transfer is also achieved through books and other paper-based documents. However, such is usually regarded as `information transfer' rather than `data transfer'. In other words, data communication and transfer is usually understood as the transfer of data by means of electronic signals between computers and other electronic equipment such as fax machines. Such data transfer can occur between electronic equipment located in different offices, organizations or countries.

2.8.9 **Data display and presentation** refers to the process of displaying and presenting data for direct human perception and interpretation. Effective data display and presentation is required in any situation when humans must interact with data through sight or hearing. Instances of such situations are when data are being presented in books and newspapers, when data are being presented on computer screens, when data are being printed out on receipts and invoices, and when spoken data are being presented at lectures or meetings. Data display and presentation is a critical last stage in the data management cycle because it occurs at the point when data are seen or heard, and immediately interpreted to gain information. The aim of data management merges with those of information management at this stage because both aim to facilitate human access to, and interpretation of, data to obtain information.

You will be learning more about each of these processes and activities in Module II of this course.

> **Exercise 2.2**
>
> Arrange in rank order (i.e. first to ninth) the data management activities described above in terms of the likelihood that they will be repeated more than once during a (data management cycle.

2.6 Information management

The differences and relationships between data, information and knowledge were explained in Unit 1. In the same manner, you should be aware of important differences and relationships between the aims and processes of data management compared to information and knowledge management.

Information management refers to activities and processes for facilitating the flow of information from various information and knowledge sources to people who desire the information. Information management aims at the effective transfer and exchange of facts, truths and ideas among individuals, organizations and communities.

Information management is firstly concerned with how to facilitate the communication of ideas from different sources of information, such as human experts, organizations, books, government documents, databases and libraries, to potential users of such information. Secondly, information management is concerned with facilitating actual interpretation and usage of the sources of information by the users.

Information management emphasizes the importance of human access to, and human interpretation, evaluation and use of the information. This is unlike data management that emphasizes the creation, manipulation, storage and transfer of data. However, because of the close relationship between data as symbols and information as the ideas conveyed by data, effective information management is invariably intertwined and facilitated by effective data management.

2.7 Knowledge management

As was explained in Unit 1, knowledge consists of a large pool of meaningfully interconnected facts, truths an ideas possessed by some individual, community, or mankind as a whole. Knowledge is usually divided into subjects, disciplines or specialties. There are also theoretical and applied aspects of knowledge.

Individuals utilize their existing knowledge in deciding how to express information with data, and also for inferring information from data. They also use their knowledge for evaluating new information, and ultimately, for making decisions toward solving human problems. Accordingly, knowledge management entails activities and processes that facilitate the growth, integration and application of ideas from various subjects and disciplines to solve human problems.

Knowledge management aims to facilitate the use of integrated ideas from different subjects to solve human problems thereby expanding knowledge further.

2.8 Data, information and knowledge management compared

Table 2.1 summarizes the purposes and sample activities in data, information and knowledge management.

What you should note from Table 2.1 is that some data management activities are usually required in support of both information and knowledge management. Knowledge management benefits from effective information management in that the latter seeks to facilitate the communication and exchange, and hence, the growth and integration of ideas among sources and centres of knowledge. In turn, information management benefits from effective data management in that the latter ensures that data from which users can derive information are created, analyzed, stored and transferred as appropriate.

Table 2.1: Comparing data, information and knowledge management

	Aims	Sample activities
Data management	To facilitate effective creation, computation and analysis, storage and retrieval, transfer and delivery of data.	Organize data in books or computers. Transfer data between locations.
Information management	To facilitate effective communication and exchange of facts and ideas from and to various knowledge stores, centres and sources such as human experts, books, databases, etc.	Identify different sources of information and knowledge such as experts, documents and databases. Facilitate access to data, information and knowledge sources by creating indexes and abstracts such sources.

| Knowledge management | To facilitate the growth and application of ideas from different disciplines for making decisions and solving human problems. | Stimulate research, creativity and innovation among researchers. Facilitate the application of ideas from diverse disciplines to solve problems. |

2.9 Conclusion

Data management activities aim to facilitate the cost-effective creation, processing and transfer of data in different contexts. However, to the extent that data serve as vehicles for conveying and inferring information, the data management activities also support the processes of information management. Also, to the extent that information flow helps to enrich knowledge, information management also supports knowledge management

2.10 Summary

In this unit, you have learnt about the nature of data management, the concept of the data management cycle, and the sequence of data management activities that are often performed in the cycle. These activities include data policy-making, data definition and structuring, data creation and collection, validation and quality control, data storage and retrieval, data analysis and summarization, data communication and transfer, data display and presentation, and data archiving and protection.

You also learnt about the purposes of information and knowledge management. The point was made that data management invariably is interwoven with information management, and that information management usually contributes to knowledge management.

2.10 Self-assessment exercises

1. Describe briefly three contexts where data are often collected in modern societies.
2. What do you understand by data validation and quality control, and why is it important in the data management cycle? Mention two methods that can be used to perform data validation and quality control.
3. Contrast data, information and knowledge management; or, discuss the statement: 'data management supports information management, which, in turn, supports knowledge management'.
4. Start a computer that uses the Microsoft Windows operating system. Write twenty sentences to describe how icons, bars, text, and colour are arranged or used in the Desktop window.

INFORMATION SYSTEMS FOR DATA MANAGEMENT

Table of Content	
3.1	Introduction
3.2	Objectives
3.3	Information systems
3.4	Data management activities of information systems
3.5	Information systems resources for data management
3.6	Data management in specific systems and contexts
3.6.1	An office as an information system
3.6.2	A pupil information system
3.7	Conclusion
3.8	Summary
3.9	Self- assessment exercises

3.1 Introduction

Welcome to Unit three. In this unit you will learn about information systems and how data management activities are performed in such systems. The aim is to consolidate your understanding and appreciation of information systems, and how the goals of information systems are invariably intertwined with the goals of data and information management.

You will also begin to learn about various real-life contexts within which data management problems are encountered and solved. The aim is to improve your understanding of such contexts, thereby preparing the ground for explaining in greater detail in subsequent units the data management activities that you learnt about in Unit 2.

3.2 Objectives

After studying this unit, you should be able to:

1. Describe the goals, key features and processes of information systems.

2. Explain how the goals of information systems are interwoven with those of data and information management.

3. Explain the data management activities involved in the input-process-storage- output communication processes of information systems.

3.3 Information systems

What is an information system? An information system may be described as a set of interdependent activities designed to provide data and/or information to people. Information systems aim to provide, or facilitate access to data and information for a particular group of people, who may be researchers, managers, students, or the public.

Before talking more about information systems however, let me explain the essential features of systems. A system is defined as a set of mutually interdependent components all contributing toward the achievement of some goal or objectives. Another way of describing a system is to say that a system comprises of objects that must work in harmony towards achieving a purpose. A good example of a system is a motor car engine. The purpose of a motor car engine is to provide mechanical energy for moving the car. Engineers construct a car engine as a set of mutually interdependent components or sub- systems which must work in harmony toward achieving the purpose of the engine whenever the engine is started. Hence, the engine is provided with an electrical sub-system, an internal combustion sub-system, a heat-to-mechanical energy conversion sub-system, a cooling sub-system, the exhaust sub-system, etc. Moreover, the car engine system itself can be shown to be a sub-system of a larger system - the motor car system, the latter comprising the engine sub-system (already described), the transmission sub-system, the steering sub-system, the braking sub-system, the electrical wiring subsystem, the passenger seating sub-system, etc. Other examples of systems are the human body system, the government system of a country, and economic system of a country, etc.

All systems share the following features:

- Goals or objectives: These give direction to the activities of a system. A system without goals or objectives is likely to perform purposeless activities, and will eventually collapse as a result of the impossibility of obtaining resources for sustaining such activities.

- Sub-systems: These are the mutually dependent components of a system. For instance, a human body is a system comprising of the nervous, respiratory, circulation, digestive and other sub-systems. The engine of a car is also a system comprising of the combustion, cooling, electrical, transmission and other systems. Each sub-system of a system can usually be regarded also as a system comprising other sub-systems, and so on.

- Environment: This comprises all other systems that do not belong to a particular system, and with which the system shares boundaries. No system can have all the resources it needs to operate independently of its environment for ever. The environment serves as a source of resources required by a system, as well as the destination for output from a system. A system needs to constantly monitor its environments for new opportunities for, or threats to, its own survival.

- Activities: A system usually must perform some physical activity in order to achieve its goals and objectives. The activities of a system can usually be divided into two main types - physical activities, and communication and information activities. Physical activities are those that involve physical work, and require physical effort or mechanical energy to accomplish. An example is the transportation of physical products or waste materials from one part of a system to another, or the physical or chemical transformation of raw materials into finished products.

- Products. Communication and information activities are those that involve the creation, storage, communication, etc., of data and/or information. All systems need to perform at least some communication and information activities (e.g., communication of information among its sub-systems). Communication and information activities are often undertaken within a system in order to ensure that the sub-systems synchronize their activities. Communication and information activities are often also undertaken between a system and its environment.

- Resources: These are required for performing physical and information activities. The resources usually include tangible and intangible things, such as space, equipment, energy, finance, time and human effort.

3.4 Data management activities of information systems

All systems, irrespective of whether they are information systems or other types of systems, need to perform information processing and communication activities in order to ensure that information is exchanged among their sub- systems. The information exchange is to ensure that the various subsystems are aware of system objectives, and perform activities toward realizing the objectives.

Furthermore, information systems in particular must also process data and information for people and other systems in their environments. This is their primary purpose, as noted earlier. In this respect, an information system is expected to create or acquire data and information from its environment, and then process the data and information toward producing other data or information for supply to other systems and people in its environment. To achieve this, an information system must perform various data and information activities.

In other words, information systems provide the settings within which data and information management activities are performed. These activities are often grouped into five major kinds (Figure 3.1)

(a) Input;
(b) Processing;
(c) Storage;
(d) Output;
(e) Communication.

Data input activities involves the inflow (i.e., input) of data to the system from other systems. This entails the acquisition or capture of data from the environment.

Data processing activities involves the transformation of data into more informative data, by aggregating, desegregating, summarizing and computing the data.

Data storage entails storing the data temporarily or permanently before, during and after processing.

Data and information output entails sending out processed data and information from the system to other systems (people, organizations, communities).

Data and information communication entails the sending and receiving of data and information among the components of a system, as well as between the system and other systems in its environment. Data communication activities are invariably performed in connection with the input, storage, processing and output activities of systems.

Environment

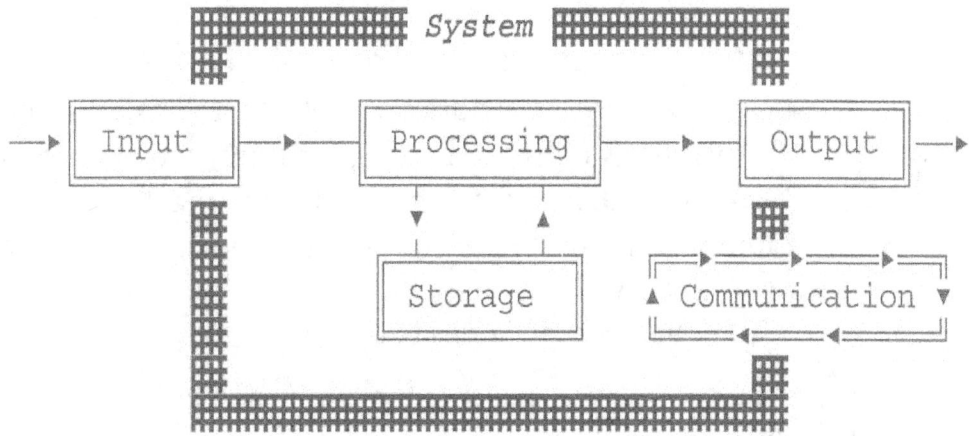

Figure 3.1 Input, Store, Processing, Output and communication Operations of an information system.

A system often must communicate with its environment in order to obtain inputs, as well as in order to deliver its outputs. Also, a system often must also communicate data among its sub-systems in order to process data, or in order to store and retrieve data from storage. System communication activities are indicated by the arrows in Figure 3.1.

3.5   Information systems resources for data management

An information system requires resources to perform and sustain its data management activities. These resources can be grouped into the following:

- Data, as raw materials for producing information, and also sometimes as output;

- People, such as data collector and data entry clerks, supervisors, managers, etc.
- Physical facilities and equipment, such as buildings and offices, computers, telephone lines, fax machines, etc.
- Organizational structure and policies, to link and control interactions between people, facilities, activities, data, etc.
- Energy, such as electricity to drive the machines, and human energy and motivation to drive people to work for the system;
- Time, because activities take time.

Each of these resources cost money, time and effort to acquire and use. This is why it is very important for information systems to adopt effective strategies and methods for data management so that the costs of data input, storage and processing can be kept low, and so that their information and data output will be very valuable to the people and systems to which they provide the output.

Exercise 3.1

Refer back to the nine data management activities in the data life-cycle described in Unit 2. Which of the activities can be classified as (i) 'input, (ii) processing, (iii) output, (iv) storage and (v) communication, and why?

3.6 Data management in specific contexts and systems

3.6.1 An office as an information system

You should note that an organization is an example of a system, with departments and units as sub-systems. Indeed, your office in which you work is also a sub-system of the organization in which your office is located within which input, storage, process, output and communication activities are also performed.

However, before you read on do the following exercise.

> **Exercise 3.2**
> Study Figure 3.2 carefully. Considering the office as a system, and list three (5) resources that can tie used for data and information: (a) input (b) storage (c) processing (d) output (e) communication.

3.6.2 Pupil information system of a primary school

Schools, colleges and universities create and maintain information systems for collecting, storing analyzing and reporting data and information about their pupils or students. Many of such information systems are completely manually operated, i.e., they do not do not involve the use of computers at all.

Let me now describe the operations of a pupil information system that primary schools often create and maintain. In such a system,

Data are collected from pupils when they register in a school for the first time. Pupils' parents are required to fill various forms for that purpose.

Hence, the forms are the means through which the pupil information system obtains data (data input). Subsequently, the forms might be kept in paper files or cabinets (data storage). Moreover, the data in the forms might be copied into note books or attendance registers (data storage). The data in the forms, notebooks or registers might then be used to calculate the total number of pupils in each class, or to arrange the names of the pupils in alphabetical order, or to calculate the total fees paid by all pupils (data processing).

During the school term, the class attendance registers will be used to record pupil's attendance (data input and data storage). Also, the marks obtained by pupils in various tests and examinations are calculated (data processing), and then recorded in note books, registers, sheets, etc. (data storage).

Finally, at the end of each school term various reports may be produced from the data that had been collected, processed and stored during the year. One such report are the pupils' report cards that show each pupils' performance during the term. The report card is produced by summarizing and calculating data from registration forms, class attendance registers, examination mark sheets, etc. The report card is an output of the pupil information system. Other reports might be prepared monthly, each term, or annually, and distributed among teachers, or sent to the local education authority (data/information communication).

Exercise 3.2

Visit a nearest primary school, and interview the Head Master/Mistress to find out what data are collected from pupils when they register at the school, and how the data are used. Ask also about that where the data are stored and processed. Study also the pupil report card used by the school.

Write twenty sentences to describe your findings. You should also include a list of the data or information that are provided on the pupil report cards produced by the school.

3.7. Conclusion

Data and information are created by people in different activities in the home, school and work place. People also come across or use data and information in different contexts. Often the process of creating or using data and information is so natural that people do not have to worry too much about the processes involved. For instance, people converse any time of the day, they write and exchange letters, they listen to lecture and take notes, and they listen to the radio or watch the television, etc. What may not be obvious to most people is that all such activities are performed within information systems.

Of course, people often do not have to worry about the concept of information system when they converse, write letters, take notes or listen to the radio. But information professionals have to. As explained earlier, an information system is a set of mutually interdependent activities designed to provide data and/or information to people. The concept of information system has been developed to enable information professionals to identify and analyze sets of mutually dependent information activities in terms of how they depend on one another, and terms of their goals, environments and resources, and in terms of the types of data and information that they produce for people.

3.8 Summary

An information system may be described as a set of interdependent activities designed to provide data and/or information to people. Information systems aim to provide, or facilitate access to data and information for a particular group of people. Information systems provide the settings within which data and information management activities are performed. These activities are often grouped into five major kinds - input, processing, storage, output and communication.

Information systems can be described or analyzed in terms of their goals or objectives that they seek to achieve, the environment in which they operate their sub-systems, the types of activities that they emphasize, and the nature of the resources they need or use to perform the activities. Finally, the concept of information systems enables information professionals to analyze separately, sets of mutually dependent information activities in terms of their objectives, activities, environments, resources, and the data and information that they acquire, create, process or produce.

3.9 Self-assessment exercises

1. What data management activities do information systems perform?

2. Explain the features of information systems and how they are designed to facilitate data/information management.
3. Describe the data management activities of any shop, social club or office of your choice.

LANGUAGES FOR DATA ORGANIZATION

	Table of Contents
4.1	Introduction
4.2	Objectives
4.3	Natural languages for data organization
4.4	Symbols, rules and usages of natural languages Scientific and other special
4.5	languages Scientific methods for
4.6	representing quantities Summary
4.9	Self-assessment
4.10	References

4.1 Introduction

In unit 3 we learnt about information systems for data management and how data management are performed in such systems. Unit 4 describes the languages for data organization where rules, symbols and usage of natural and special languages will be discussed.

4.2 Objectives

After studying this unit, you should be able to:

1. Explain the nature and importance of natural and special languages for social communication and data creation.

2. Describe how the symbols, rules and usages of a language determine what and how data can be created for expressing information.

4.3 Natural languages for data organization

Individuals usually create data to describe whatever they might know already, or might have seen, heard, tasted, smelt or touched. In other words, they create data to express information. Sometimes, they are free to select and combine symbols that they understand to create the data, especially when they do not intend to communicate the data and the associated information to others. For instance, a person might use secret symbols to express information in a secret diary or map so that no one else may understand the information implied by the data.

In most cases however, people create data for conveying information to others. In such instances, an individual has to be careful about what symbols are used to communicate information. Usually, the symbols must be selected and arranged in a way that others can understand. This is the rationale for the existence of natural languages such as English, French, Hausa, Igbo and Yoruba that can be used to create data for expressing information. In other words, natural languages are the standard vehicles for social communication within societies.

You will of course be aware that people differ in their ability to communicate in different languages. In the same manner, people differ in their abilities to correctly use a particular language to express information with data. Similarly, people differ in their abilities to interpret information from data that has been created with a particular language.

4.4 Natural language symbols, rules and usages

An individual might be described as 'illiterate', meaning that the person cannot read or write in a *particular language*. Please note the words in italics. This is to say that the person cannot read or write in the language. This is the same as saying that the person does not understand the symbols or data that are used in the language to express information. Similarly other persons might be described as 'barely literate', or 'highly literate' in a language.

The important point to note is that the ability of an individual to use a particular language to express information with data, as well as the ability to interpret information from data in the language depends on that individual's knowledge of the symbols, rules and usage of the language.

So, what are the symbols, rules and usages of natural languages?

Natural languages that are written invariably have alphabetic symbols, which, when combined in various ways can be used to form words and sentences. In addition, there are also special symbols such as comma, full stop, question marks, etc. Languages also have rules of spelling, grammar and punctuation that people are expected to use when using the language to create data for expressing information. Hence, 'elephant' can be recognized as a word in English language, but 'elephant' is not. Similarly, the phrase 'the pot is in the bucket' can be easily interpreted by a person literate in English language, but not so easily the phrase 'pot the is the bucket in'.

Of course, the main reason why human societies require that data must be created in accordance with these rules of language is in order to reduce or eliminate the chances of misunderstanding between the creators and interpreters of data. Such misunderstanding might then lead to differences between the information expressed by creators of data and the information that interpreters can obtain from the data.

Accordingly, written natural languages often have:

(a) Alphabets and other special symbols (e.g. comma), which are the symbols that can be used for creating and recording data to express information.

(b) Spelling rules that guide how alphabetic symbols may be combined to form words;

(c) Grammar rules that guide how words could be combined to form sentences;

(d) Rules, conventions or styles of structure that guide how sentences can be strung together to form paragraphs, and how paragraphs can be arranged when writing for different audiences;

(e) Conventions or rules as to the likely meanings that can be implied by different combinations of symbols, words, etc.

(f) Rules and conventions as to how to pronounce combinations of symbols, such as words, in the language.

(g) Dictionaries specifying the recognized symbols, spelling, grammar and usages in the language, as well as the meanings of the symbols and combinations of symbols. Dictionaries often also provide guidance on how combinations of symbols, for example words, should be pronounced.

> **Exercise 4.1**
>
> Get hold of an English language dictionary, and' explain the types of information that is provided for each word in the dictionary.

4.5 Scientific and other special languages

People belonging to different cultures often develop different languages or versions of natural languages. For instance, some people of England speak, write and understand a type of English language referred to as "Queen's English", while people in some parts of West Africa speak, write and understand "pidgin English".

In addition, special languages are also sometimes developed by and for special communities of people, such as scientists, specialized professions, or for specialized purposes as you will learn later on in this course. For instance, chemical, biological and medical scientists have developed various scientific languages for naming various types of objects. Hence, what is known as 'common salt' in natural English language is referred to as 'sodium chloride' by the chemists. Similarly, you probably learnt in your agricultural science class that 'white yam' is referred to as 'dioscorea rotundata' by the biologists. Hence, the biologists, chemists and other scientists are trained in how to use such special languages to create data. Of course, such special languages, just like natural languages, have their peculiar symbols, rules and usages.

The scientific and cultural disciplines and professions have, overtime developed and begetted unto mankind the following additional language symbols, rules and usages:

(a) Numeric symbols (0, 1, 2 ...), as well as rules on how the symbols can be combined to express quantitative information (e.g., 102.237 or 13.4 metres, or 34 F). Hence, 100 is considered to be exactly ten times larger than 10, and 10 is considered to be ten times larger than 1.

(b) Pictorial and graphic symbols, such as lines, dots, and the like, that can be used to create image data, such as maps, cartoons, line graphs, drawings, paintings, etc. The Chinese and Japanese, for instance use graphic symbols to represent information.

(c) Conventions as to the best way to arrange numerical and pictorial symbols in data tables, charts, mathematical formula, maps, dictionaries, indexes and abstracts, etc.

(d) Conventions as to how to arrange or organize data symbols, such as words, numbers, pictures, etc., its various formats, such as resumes, technical reports, application letters, etc.

4.5 Scientific methods for representing quantities

You are of course aware that information about quantities can be expressed with either words or figures. Hence, 'one hundred and ten' could also be written as 'I 10'.

Most literate people know about the decimal number and counting system, which involves the use of the 0, 1 ...9, in various combinations to express integers (e.g. 1, 23, 567, -12 ...) as well as fractional numbers (1.237, -12.67, 0.000212). Most people also know how to count in units, tens, hundredths, and so on.

Scientists have also developed other methods for expressing quantitative information with data. Firstly, there is the so-called scientific notation for expressing numbers. Hence, the number '102.23 7' is often expressed in scientific notation as $1.02237E02$.

In case you have forgotten, or had never learnt, about the scientific notation. This is a short explanation of how scientific numbers are derived from ordinary numbers.

The scientific notation is derived from a given number by applying the following two basic rules:

Move the decimal point a number of spaces from its original position in the given number so that the original number is in the form of a derived number 'N.NNNN', where the first N before the point is any of the positive or negative digits (1,2,3,   9,-1,-2...-9), and the other N's could be any positive

digit (0, 1, 2 9).

Applying this rule means that:

Given number		Derived number
1234	becomes	1.234;
-456.3	becomes	-4.563
12.66	becomes	1.266
0.238	becomes	2.39
0.000987	becomes	9.87

(ii) Find the number of times the derived number must be multiplied by ten to get the original given number. Put another way, find the power of 10 with which the derived number must be multiplied to get the original given number.

Applying this second rule, we find that

1.234 must be multiplied by 10^3 (10 raised to power 3) to obtain the original number 1234.

Similarly,

-456.3	=	-4.563×10^2
12.66	=	1.266×10^1
0.238	=	2.390×10^{-1}
0.000987	=	9.870×10^{-4}

Note however that another way of saying '10 raised to a certain positive or negative power' is to say '10 exponent the positive or negative power'. Hence, the above equations can be rewritten as

-456.3	=	-4.563×10^2	=	$-4.563E+02$
12.66	=	1.266×10^1	=	$1.266E+01$
0.238	=	2.390×10^{-1}	=	$2.390E-01$
0.000987	=	9.870×10^{-4}	=	$9.870E-04$

The numbers on the left are decimal numbers expressed in the way literate people understand, whereas the numbers on the extreme right are also decimal data, but expressed in scientific notation. In other words, scientists can choose to create and organize numbers in either the ordinary way or the scientific way. You should know both ways because you are learning to become a computer or communication scientist, or a data manager.

Now do the following exercises for practice:

Exercise 4.2

1. Explain how the number '1.02237.E'02' is the same as 102.237.
2. Express the following s scientific: notation:

   (a) 12.44

   (b) -676.3

   (c) 0.0234

   Find out if the following numbers' are equivalent:
3.
   (a) 1.555E+03   =   1550

   (b) 3.331E-02   =   .0003331

   (c) -67.38   =   -6.738E-01

   (d) -127.22   =   -1.2722E+02

Finally, scientists sometimes use other number systems than the decimal number system. These number systems may use either less or more symbols than the ten symbols (0, 1, 2 ...9) of the decimal number system. In particular, in computing you will come across the binary number system which you probably learnt about in high school. The binary number system uses only two types of digits, 0 and 1, to express quantitative information. Hence, instead of writing numbers such as 13, 129, 9999, 20.5 as is done in the decimal system, these numbers are represented instead by various combinations of zeros and ones. For instance, the number 13 in the decimal system will be represented by the number 1101 in the binary system. Similarly, the number 129 in the decimal system will be represented by the number 10000001 in the binary system.

The binary system is important in computing because computers are designed to process, store and transmit data in the form of binary numbers and signals. You will learn more about the binary system of representing quantitative information in Unit 5 of this course.

4.6 Conclusion

You should be able to recall from Unit 1 that data were described as 'facts, information, statistics, or the like, either historical or derived by calculation or experimentation'.

In conclusion, human communities create and use different languages for expressing information with data, and also for interpreting information from data. Data were described in Unit 1 as comprising written words, numbers and other symbols that have been used to describe objects. Hence, data are created when we write or record information with a language. This is the same as expressing information with data.

Finally, it is important to note that data created with a language can take both written and spoken forms. The act of writing on say paper in a language creates data in the language. That act of writing is a data recording process. Similarly, words can also be recorded as they are spoken, thereby creating recorded sound data that can be listened to, for obtaining information.

4.7 Summary

In this unit, you have learnt about the importance of languages in social communication, and how the process of using a language to express information leads to the creation of data.

Some natural languages can be written, and data are created when the written forms of such languages are used to express information. Moreover, even when a natural language is spoken, data are created and stored when the speech is recorded on some media, such as a cassette tape.

Languages range from natural languages to special languages. Among the special languages are those developed by different scientists for expressing information? Among the specialized scientific methods or languages for expressing information with data are the decimal number and counting system, use of scientific notation to express numbers, use of scientific names for common objects, and the binary number system that is used by computer systems for creating, processing, storing, transmitting and interpreting data.

4.8 Self-assessment exercises

1. Explain the importance of languages in social communication.

2. What are the common characteristics of languages?

3. Describe the kinds of information that are provided in a dictionary of any language of your choice.

DATA REPRESENTATION IN THE COMPUTER

Table of Contents	
5.1	Introduction
5.2	Objectives
5.3	How data are input and represented in computers
5.4	The binary number system
5.5	Addition and subtraction of binary numbers
5.6	Converting between decimal and binary numbers
5.7	How computers use binary numbers to represent data
5.8	How computers represent images and sound
5.9	Conclusion
5.9	Summary
5.10	Self-assessment exercises

5.1 Introduction

Computers are now used in all aspects of human endeavor - in the home, at school, and at work. Computers are machines that have been designed to accept data, to store, process and communicate the data, and produce other data. Computers can capture, process and transmit data much faster, more accurately, and more consistently than humans. Computers can also store vast quantities of data in very small media such as computer tapes and disks. For example, it is possible for a computer to store the data contents of a 200-page book on one single flat diskette measuring 3.5 inches square. Computers are rapidly replacing human in various activities that demand very fast comparison, computation and arrangement of data, or very fast transmission of data from one location to another. Computers, in the form of robots, are also being introduced to do hazardous or boring physical work, such as exploring the surface of the moon, welding vehicle chassis in a vehicle factory, or saying 'Hello, welcome' to customers as they enter a restaurant.

In the previous unit we explained how people use natural and scientific languages to express information with data, and also to infer information from data. In view of the importance of computers in the information age, you should also understand the mechanisms and rules that computer uses to create, process, store, and output data.

In other words, you need to understand how data are organized and processed by computers. Accordingly, you need to understand how computer create, store, organize, process and transmit data. This is what you will be learning in this unit.

Literate people are taught how to count in units, tens, and so on and to write statements or data in various languages using different types of alphabets, numbers and other types of characters. In addition, people see things around them, watch movies, listen to music and human speech, etc. All these are symbols that humans understand, because they are selected from human languages and cultures.

Computers are designed to mimic human beings in terms of the ability to accept different combinations of alphabetical, numeric and other characters as input, and to produce these same characters as output. Computers are designed to do this not for themselves, but only for the sake of humans. Unlike humans, computers make use of combinations of only two types of digits (0 and 1) to represent, process, store and communicate whatever characters are supplied to it by humans. In other words, the computer makes use of combinations of the two digits to represent all types of data - alphabetical, numerical and special characters, words, numbers, sound, images, etc.

In this Unit you will learn how computers, which can only store and process bits, can also accept or produce other forms of data such as words, real numbers, images or pictures, sound, etc.

5.2 Objectives

After studying this unit, you should be able to:

1. Explain the binary number system, and how to add binary numbers;

2. How computers use signals representing binary digits or bits to represent alphabetic, numeric and other characters.

3. How images and pictures are captured and represented by computers.

4. How sound and voice are captured and represented by computers.

5.3 How data are input and represented in computers

You must have learnt in your GS###: Computer Fundamentals course that the process of introducing data into a computer system is known as data input. However, other terms that are often also used are data entry, or data capture. The opposite of data input is data output. Moreover, computers process, store and communicate data within and among themselves.

Data are input to a computer through input equipment or devices connected to the computer's central processing unit (CPU). Among such devices are:

- Keyboard, for entering alphabetical, numerical and special characters;

- Mouse (for indicating and selecting options from menus displayed on a computer monitor);
- Scanners (for taking pictures of paper documents);

- Digital cameras (for taking photographs of objects); microphones (for sound and voice), etc.

The input devices perform the task of detecting signals produced by the action a computer operator, such as the press of a key on the keyboard, or the movement of a mouse, or the clicking of a digital camera, or the act of speaking into a microphone. The input devices immediately code the incoming signals into electrical pulses that are transmitted through some connecting wires to the CPU.

The inputs devices are designed to transmit sequences of combinations of high and low electronic pulses. These pulses are what the CPU understands. In other words, each input device is able to communicate with the CPU in a language of electronic pulses. In other words, any data introduced into a computer through an input device, be it the letter 'a' typed on the keyboard, or a sound received by a microphone, or a picture taken with a camera, etc., is translated by the input device into some appropriate combination and sequences of electronic pulses which are transmitted to the CPU. On receiving the sequence of electronic pulses, the CPU will then interpret the signals to determine what original signals the electronic pulses represent, whether an 'a', or a particular sound, or a particular image.

In other words, the CPU and the input (as well as output) devices use a common language of electronic pulses to exchange data. Accordingly, data are represented in computer systems not in the form of natural language symbols, but in the form of electronic symbols, ie. Electronic pulses. As noted above, the electronic pulses are of just two kinds, low and high, and are represented by low and high electrical voltages respectively.

To recap, CPUs and input and output devices are only able to understand just two types of symbols, either low or high voltage pulses or nothing else. By contrast, human beings use a wide variety of symbols (alphabetical, numerical, special, pictorial, etc.) to express information with data. It was precisely in order to bridge the gap in the number of symbols used by humans (many symbols) and computer devices (only two symbols) that early computer engineers and scientists adopted a data coding system to be used by computer devices to translate data in human languages into equivalent data that the devices can understand, and vice versa.

You will recall that we briefly mentioned the binary number system in Unit 4, and that the binary number system uses only two types of digits (0 and 1). Accordingly, since computer devices could process only two types of symbols (low and high voltage pulses), the binary number system was adopted as a convenient system to be used by computer devices for coding, processing and communicating data within and among themselves.

5.4 The binary number system

You probably learned about the binary number system in high school. But if you did not, or you have forgotten, here is an introduction. However, in order to promote your understanding, let us review the decimal system with which you are very familiar.

The decimal system has ten symbols or digits (0, 1, 2... 9). Hence, to represent increasingly bigger units of numbers we begin at 0, and count through 1 to 9, at which point we run out of digits. The next number is nine plus one, and to represent it we write a 1 and then a 0 to get 10. What the 10 means is that we now have one of tens and zero of units. We then continue cycling through the remaining digits again, hence, 11, 12, and 19. The last number, 19, means one of tens and nine of units. The next number is then written as 20, meaning 2 tens and zero units. And so on. Similarly, the next number after 99 is 100, meaning one of hundreds and zero of units, and 1000 means one of thousands and zero of units. And so on.

Accordingly, a number such as 1234 actually means one of thousand plus two of hundreds, plus 3 of tens, and plus 4 of units:

$$
\begin{array}{r}
1000 \\
200 \\
30 \\
4 \\
\hline
1234 \\
\hline
\end{array}
$$

In other words, in the decimal system we count in units, and multiples of tens

- the ten digits of the decimal number system. Another way to say this is that in the decimal system we count in base 10. This is the familiar number system that is used to represent, and also add, subtract, multiply and divide quantities. Of course you learned about this system as early as in primary school.

Now let us see how rules for representing quantities in the binary number system is very similar (but not identical) to that of the decimal number system.

The binary number system has only two symbols or digits, 0 and 1. Hence, to represent increasingly bigger units of numbers we begin at 0, and then 1, at which point we run out of digits. The next number is one plus one, and to represent it we write a 1 and then a 0 to get 10. Note however, what the 10 here means is that we now have one of and zero of units. The next number will the be 11, that is one of and one of units. Thereafter, the next number will be 100, meaning one of fours and zero of twos and zeros of units. We then continue counting 101, and then 111. The next number will be 1000, meaning one of eights, zero of fours, zero of twos and zero of units. Next will be 1001, 1011, 1111, 10000, 10001. Now, what is the meaning of the last number? It means one of sixteens, zero of eights, zero of fours, zero of twos and one of units.

In other words, in the binary number system we count in units, and multiples of twos - the two digits of the binary number system. Another way to say this is that in the binary system we count in base 2.

This is the way the binary number system is built up, from zero numbers to very large numbers. Hence, a binary number such as 1001010 can be decomposed as

1 of 64's	=	2^6	=	(i.e., 2 raised to power 6)
0 of 32's	=	2^5	=	(i.e., 2 raised to power 5)
0 of 16's	=	2^4	=	(i.e., 2 raised to power 4)
1 of 8's	=	2^3	=	(i.e., 2 raised to power 3)

0 of 4's   = 2^2 =   (i.e., 2 raised to power 2)
1 of 2's   = 2^1 =   (i.e., 2 raised to power 1)
0 of 1's   = 2^0 =   (i.e., 2 raised to power 0)

5.5 Addition and subtraction of binary numbers

Binary numbers can be added, subtracted, multiplied and divided, and the procedures are very similar to that used for decimal numbers. Consider for example, the following addition:

11000
+ 111
———

11000
———

The procedure is that we begin the addition from the right most column. Addition one and one gives one of twos and zero of units. Hence, we write 0 under the column and carry over one of twos to the next column to the left. The process is repeated until the addition is complete.

Procedures similar to those used in subtracting, multiplying and dividing decimal numbers are used for subtracting, multiplying and dividing binary numbers.

Exercise 5.1

Perform the following addition,
And subtractions:

(a) 100001 + 1 1 1 1

(b) 10101 + 10111011

(c) 1000011 + 1

(d) 1000011 - 1

(e) 1111111 - MM]

(f) 1111111 - 100001

5.6 Converting between decimal and binary numbers

You know already that in the decimal system, numbers are counted from zero upwards, in units, tens, hundreds, thousands' and so on. Hence the first twenty numbers, as well as a few other selected numbers are shown in Table 5.1

Table 5.1: Equivalence between some decimal and binary numbers

Decimal number	Binary number equivalent
0	0
1	1
2	10
3	11
4	100
5	101
6	110
7	111
8	1000
9	1001
10	1011
16	10000

20	10100
30	11110
32	100000
64	1000000
99	1100011
100	1100100
128	10000000

What you learn is how to covert decimal numbers to binary numbers, and vice versa.

(a) Conversion of decimal numbers to binary

The procedure is illustrated with the following example. Given a decimal number 235:

235 (in decimal) =

1 of 128 (or 1 of 2^7) +

1 of 64 (or 1 of 2^6) +

1 of 32 (or 1 of 2^5) +

0 of 16 (or 0 of 2^4) +

1 of 8 (or 1 of 2^3) +

0 of 4 (or 0 of 2^2) +

1 of 2 (or 1 of 2^1) +

1 of 1 (or 1 of 2^0).

Thereafter add up the binary number equivalent of each line on the right of the equation, hence:

10000000 +
1000000 +
100000 +

```
       00000 +
        1000 +
         000 +
          10 +
           1
       _____

   11101011  (in binary)
   _____
```

In other words, the procedure is:

(1) Find the highest power of two that can be taken from the given decimal number with a remainder (zero is a remainder).

(ii) Find the next lower multiples or powers of two, which can be taken from the remainder in step (i);

(iii) Repeat step (ii) until you cycle through all the multiples or powers of two lower than that found in step (i);

(iv) Add up the binary number equivalents of the different powers of two obtained from steps (i) to (iii).

(b) Conversion of binary numbers to decimal numbers

Procedure is illustrated with the following example. Given a binary number 1100011, expand the number as follows:

$1 \times 2^6 =$ 64 (in decimal) +

$1 \times 2^5 =$ 32 (in decimal) +

$0 \times 2^4 =$ 0 (in decimal) +

$0 \times 2^3 =$ 0 (in decimal) +

$0 \times 2^2 =$ 0 (in decimal) +

$1 \times 2^1 =$ 2 (in decimal) +

$1 \times 2^0 =$ 1 (in decimal)

----

99 (in decimal).

You should confirm the accuracy of the conversion by referring to Table 5.1

Exercise 5.2

(a) Convert the following decimal numbers to binary numbers: 666. 300, 17, 222, 255,

(b) Convert the following binary numbers to decimal numbers: 1000011 1110 1.101, 10000000001, 1 0 1 0 1010.

5.7 How computers use binary numbers to represent data

We have already explained in section 5.3 that computer devices are only able to process only two types of symbols, i.e., high and low electronic pulses. In other words, computers process, store and communicate combinations and sequences of high and low pulses. Hence, binary numbers were adopted by computer engineers and scientists for representing the combinations and sequences of high and low electronic pulses understood by computers.

Accordingly, different types of binary coding systems have been developed for coding into binary numbers the various human data symbols that might be entered into a computer through various input devices. Most computers use a binary coding system known as the American Standard Code for Information Exchange (ASCII) developed by the American National Standard Institute (ANSI).

The way in which some human language symbols, such as digits, alphabetical and special characters are coded in the ASCII standard is shown in Table 5.2. Each different character is given a decimal number, as well as a binary number. The decimal numbers are intended for use by humans in specifying which characters being sent into the computer, whereas the binary numbers are by computers processing, storing and communication data. Computers do this by processing, storing and transmitting combinations and sequences of high and low electronic pulses corresponding to the binary numbers assigned for each character

Table 5.2: Some ASCII characters and their decimal and binary code

Character	Decimal code	Binary code
Some special characters		
Space	32	0100000
#	35	0100011
$	36	0100100
%	37	0100101
&	38	0100111
,	44	0101100
Some digits		
0	48	0110000
1	49	0110001
2	50	0110010
3	51	0110011

Some uppercase letters

A	65	1000001
B	66	1000010
C	67	1000011

Some lowercase letters

a	97	1100001
b	98	1100010
c	99	1100011

Accordingly, typing the letter 'a' on the keyboard sets in motion the following events:

(i) 'a' is typed;

(ii) The keyboard notes this and converts the 'a' into the binary number 1100001. It then sends a sequence of electronic pulses patterned after the digits in the binary number to the CPU.

(iii) The CPU interprets the pulses, stores the signals in temporary memory, and then send the same pattern of signals to the computer monitor (an output device)

(iv) The monitor interprets the incoming pattern of pulses, and interprets them to mean 'a', which it displays on the screen.

Exercise 5.3

Use Table 5.2 to do this exercise. Suppose that a particular brand of keyboard is designed to send signals representing individual key presses to CPU the following format: each key press is followed by space. ,Using this format, write out the sequence of binary numbers that the keyboard will send as electronic pulses to the CPU for the following keys pressed on the keyboard:

(a) Abc

(b) 341

(c) 25B

5.8 How computers represent images and sound

We have so far explained how computers use electronic pulses to represent, process, store and transmit binary data using the ASCII system. But how do computers represent images or graphics that might have been captured by a digital camera or a scanner, or drawn with graphics software? [Note: A Graphic software is a computer program, such as Microsoft paint, that can be used to draw lines, curves, charts, maps, and paintings].

Basically, all what you need to know at this level is that the input devices that are used to capture or create graphic images are designed to code the image as sequences of binary numbers, which are then transmitted as binary electronic pulses to the CPU. Similarly, sound captured by a microphone is transmitted as a continuous stream of binary electronic pulses to the CPU.

Exercise 5.4

Visit a computer or business bureau centre near you to find out (if you had not previously), how a scanner, a digital camera, and a microphone can be or are attached to computers, and also how they are used to capture images and sound.

5.9 Conclusion

In unit 4 we explained that human societies use natural and special languages to express information with data. We also noted that languages have symbols, rules for combining the symbols, and the meaning that various combinations of symbols convey. Languages also often have dictionaries that contain information on how the language could or should be used. In the same manner, the ASCII system is like a language which most computers use to determine what binary signals to process, store and transmit in order to input, transform or output symbols in natural languages such as alphabetical, numerical and special characters. Similar binary numbers and signals are used for processing sound and image data.

5.10 Summary

In this unit, you have learnt about how computer devices code, process, store and transmit data. Humans use a wide variety of symbols, including alphabetical, numerical, special and pictorial symbols. Humans also use the decimal number system for counting in units, tens, hundreds, and so on. By contrast, computers can only understand and process only two kinds of symbols – high and low voltage pulses. Hence, computer engineers and scientists adopted the binary system for use by computer devices to code the wide variety of human symbols.

The binary number system uses only two symbols – 0 and 1 – in different combinations and sequences to represent quantities. Binary numbers can be added, subtracted and multiplied, much in the same way as decimal numbers. Binary numbers can also be converted into decimal numbers, and vice versa.

The different symbols used by humans for creating data such as alphabetical, numeric and special characters are represented by both decimal and binary numbers in the American Standard Codes for Information Interchange (ASCII) developed by the American Standards Institute (ANSI), and most computers use such codes to determine the binary digits and electronic pulses to process, store or transmit. This is basically how data are represented in computers.

5.11 Self-assessment exercises

1. Explain how numbers are added in the binary system.

2. Explain how alphabetical, numerical and special characters are coded as binary numbers by computer systems.

3. Describe how a scanner is used to capture images for input into a computer system.

4. Use Table 5.2 to figure out the ASCII decimal and binary numbers representing the following
   (a) Numbers 4 through 9;
   (b) Uppercase letters C-Z;
   (c) Lowercase letters c-z.

DATA PLANNING AND POLICY MAKING

Table of Contents	
6.1	Introduction
6.2	Objectives
6.3	Planning for data
6.4	Information resource management
6.5	Data and information policies
6.6	Example: Data policy issues in data collection
6.7	Data policy manuals
6.8	Data planning and policy-making requirements
6.9	Conclusion
6.10	Summary
6.11	Self-assessment exercises

6.1 Introduction

There is a saying that 'if you fail to plan, you will be planning to fail'. This is similar to the idiom that says 'look before you leap'. The wisdom in both sayings is that you are more likely to succeed than fail in an activity when you make and implement plans for it. This is particularly true when the activity requires outlays of money, time and effort, and when failure can be very costly. So is data organization and management.

You learned in Unit 3 that data management activities are usually performed by information systems, and that the activities usually demand the use of resources such as data, people, equipment, energy and time. Of course, the more data and information that are created or acquired by a system for processing, storage, output and communication, the more resources that will be required. But resources are not free, and some resources, such as time, are fixed. Accordingly, various procedures, policies and plans may be established by different information systems to guide and regulate the processes of data creation, management and use.

In this unit you will learn about some of these guidelines and policies. You will learn about the nature of policies that organizations and information systems often establish to guide their data management activities. You will also learn about the importance of making and implementing rules, plans and policies for data organization and management.

6.2 Objectives

After studying this unit, you should be able to:

1. Explain the role of data planning in the process of data management.
2. Describe aims of information resources management.
3. Discuss the importance of data and information policies in data management.
4. Describe the types of information that data policy manuals usually contain.

6.3 Planning for data

The planning of any human activity invariably aims to answer, before the commencement of the activity, the following five basic questions:

- Why should the activity be done?
- Where should the activity be done?
- When should the activity be done?
- What tasks must be done in the activity?
- Who should do which tasks in the activity?

Planning involves obtaining prior information to enable the planner to answer each of the above questions.

Data management activities consume valuable resources, and hence, must be planned effectively to ensure success and avoid mistakes and wastage. In other words, planning for data management requires that one finds prior answers to such questions as:

- What information should be produced for various people who need information in an organization or information system, and why?
- What data should be collected, stored, analyzed, communicated, etc., toward producing the required information?

- How should the data be collected, stored, analyzed, communicated, etc? When should the data be collected, stored, analyzed, communicated, etc? Who should be responsible for the different activities in the data management cycle?

Exercise 3.1

(a) Answer the following questions: Do you:

(i) Always keep letters and greetings cards that you receive from friends?

(ii) Keep copies of letters that you hand write?

(iii) Keep copies of official letters that you write?

(iv) Keep your books always well arranged on your table shelves?

(v) Always carefully read over your answers in an examination?

(vi) Frequently change methods you use for obtaining information?

(vii) You use radio/TV to obtain information more than newspapers?

(viii) Share information with friends immediately you get it?

(ix) Often try to confirm the accuracy of any information that you receive from: Your friends? Your parents? Your teachers? Newspaper?

(x) Arrange the following potential sources of data and information in the decreasing order in which you prefer to use them: books, newspapers, teachers, internet, personal notebooks of your course mates, radio, TV, parents, etc

(b) Use your answers in (a) to explain your own personal policies toward data and information in your life.

6.4 Information resource management

As explained in Unit 2, data management processes are often intertwined with those concerned with information management. The reason is that data are the vehicles through which people convey information, and through which people obtain information.

Information is nowadays, recognized as a vital resource that can be used and re-used to improve the knowledge of individuals and organizations. Hence, information is now regarded as a resource, just like natural, human and financial resources had been for a long time.

The recognition of information as a vital resource has given rise to a branch of management known as information resource management (IRM). The basic idea of IRM is that information resources should be properly and carefully managed by competent information professionals, just as finance has been managed by accountants for many years. The main ideas championed by IRM professionals are:

- That information resources include information and data, as well as the technologies for creating, acquiring, storing, processing and communicating data, and for producing and using information.
- That information and data are very valuable because they cost money to acquire, process and use, and because they can be used to improve the value of human, financial, natural and knowledge resources.

- Those managerial principles must be devised for managing information resources. Hence, all data, information and knowledge management activities must be carefully planned, performed and evaluated to minimize their cost and to maximize their benefits to organizations and information systems.

- That information resources must be managed by qualified information professionals. In other words, qualified information professionals and knowledgeable people should plan and manage information resources.

- The basic argument of people who champion information resources management is that organizations and information system will be better able to develop and manage their information and data resources when they accept and apply the above principles. Do you believe them?

6.5 Data and information policies

A policy is a set of statements that describe the circumstances, objectives and constraints to be followed by people in an organization or information system concerning a particular activity or issue.

You would remember, for instance, some policies of the primary school that you attended some years ago. You would recall that there were rules or policies regarding punctuality and lateness at school, regarding the behaviour expected of pupils, regarding punishment for various offence, regarding the roles of teachers, parents, etc. You would recall also that some of these school rules were written and pasted on notice boards, and that many others are not written but were nevertheless known and respected by pupils, teachers and parents. In a similar way, data management policies are usually formulated by organizations and information systems to explain why and how the various data management activities should be performed.

Data policies are usually formulated to ensure that only potentially useful data are created or acquired for processing and management by an organization or information system. Potentially useful data are those from which more useful data or information can be produced.

6.6 Example: Data policy issues in data collection

Appropriate data policies can be formulated to guide each of the activities in a data management cycle that was first introduced in Unit 2. Maybe you should review Unit 2 now to refresh your memory.

Here we will illustrate the basic objective of data policies by looking at the issues that are usually addressed by data policies for one of the data management activities - data collection and acquisition. Data collection and acquisition activities are performed by information systems to obtain data for subsequent storage, communication and processing to produce information.

Data policies for data collection and acquisition will often provide guidelines and other helpful information that can be used by people in organizations and information systems for answering the following questions:

Why should certain types of data be collected, acquired or created?

(a) The usual reason for collecting or acquiring data of any kind is in order to enable subsequent processing and interpretation of the data to produce information and other more valuable data required by people (referred to as information users) within and outside an organization or information system. Users need information either to improve their knowledge, make decisions or solve problems. In other words, the types of information that users would require usually depend on such things as the types of subjects they are studying, the type of work they do, the issues they have to decide on, and the problems they have to solve, and sometimes, the types of leisure activities they engage in.

(b) What specific types of data should the organization or information system collect, acquire or create?

The data policy would explain data to be collected, should be collected or created only on specific groups of people, certain types of organizations, or certain subjects, activities, events, places, etc. The policy might also require that the data to be collected or acquired should meet certain minimum standards of accuracy, detail, timeliness, etc. As noted above, the policy would justify the specific types of data to be collected or acquired on the basis of the information that will be produced from the data for users by the organization or information system.

(c) What symbols should be used to create data, and/or in what format and from what media should data be collected or acquired?

As explained in Module 1, data can be created or acquired in numeric, textual, graphical, pictorial and sound symbols and formats. For example, an event can be described in words, or recorded in a video tape, an audio tape, or in a series of photographs. The data policy will seek to provide guidelines as to which formats should be used for acquiring or creating data for the organization or information system. The reason is that each of the different formats in which data can be created or acquired requires different technologies and equipment.

(d) From what sources should data be collected or acquired?

Data can be collected from various sources. Data can be collected from people in a questionnaire survey, or by means of forms which certain people might be required to fill when they request for or purchase goods or services. Such data are referred to as primary data. However, data can also be extracted from books, magazines, newspapers, computers and the Internet. Such data are referred to as secondary data. Data might also be collected from within and outside an organization or information system. These are internal and external data respectively. The data policy will seek to explain the types of data and information sources that should be emphasized by the organization or system.

(e) When and how frequently should data be acquired, collected or created?

A data policy will sometimes explain how frequently certain data should be collected - whether hourly, daily, weekly, monthly, annually, etc. The policy may also specify when certain data should be collected. For instance, candidates in an examination are often required to fill attendance forms at the start of the examination and not after the examination. Can you guess the reason for this?

What should be the functions or responsibility of different organizational units in the data capture, acquisition and creation processes?

Data collection is usually performed by different organizational units or systems components. For example, at the start of an academic year or semester, students are usually required by their schools and colleges to fill forms indicating what courses they desire to take in their respective departments, and are at the same time also required to fill forms and pay tuition and other fees in the accounts department. They may also be required to fill forms in order to check into hostels of residence. Hence, data policies often specify the responsibilities of the different organizational units and personnel in respect of various data collection activities.

The above questions and the explanations provided underneath them focus only on data collection and acquisition activities. Of course, similar questions and explanations can be given in respect of each of the other data management activities. You should at this point write out questions similar to those above for at least one of the other data management activities described in Unit 2, such as: data analysis and summarization, data storage and retrieval, data protection and archiving, data communication and transfer, etc. This is an exercise for you (Exercise 3.1).

> **Exercise 4.1**
>
> Write out sample data protection and archiving questions that a data management policy might provide to assist people in an organization or system to answer.
>
> [Hint: Try to replace the words 'acquisition', 'collection' and. 'creation' with "protection' and "archiving" in the questions provided in the text.]

6.7 Data policy manuals

A data policy is a basic guide to action that sets the boundaries within which data management activities are to take place. Most organizations and information systems establish general principles to regulate their data and information activities. A policy may be written or unwritten. The advantage of a written policy is that it can easily be referred to in case of disagreement about appropriate and inappropriate activities.

A written policy is usually referred to as a policy manual. The following are some of the advantages of policy manuals. Policy manuals

- Provide plans of action in respect of most data management issues, activities, events and problems;
- Forces people within an organization or information system to think carefully through whatever they want to do with data;
- Enable people within an information system to perform their respective data management functions and tasks in a standardized, consistent manner;
- Often establish data quality control points which often help to ensure data quality; help to preserve ways of doing things, even though employees may change;
- Can be used as material for training and job orientation of new employees;
- Serve as a starting point for thinking about how to improve on how data management activities can be improved within an organization and information system.

Table 6.1 shows some sample statements that a written data management policy manual might contain.

Table 6.1 Five sample statements from the Data Policy of Organization X

1.1 This data policy should be used as a guide in all departments of this organization for determining the data to be acquired, collected or created.

1.2 Data to' be collected should also be determined 'through, periodic surveys of the actual and potential information need of middle and top, level managers. Such surveys should be conducted every five years.

1.3 As far as practicable, data should be immediately captured unto appropriate storage media at the point' where they are being created.

1.4 Employees who are responsible for data creation, capture and acquisition should periodically be trained on their responsibilities in ensuring that data meet the minimum standards of accuracy.

6.8 Data planning and policy-making requirements

Effective data planning and policy-making in an organization or information system demands that people in the organization or information system

(a) Accept the importance of data, information and knowledge activities, and the necessity to properly manage the activities;

(b) Establish specific policies to guide and regulate various data management activities within the organization or information system;

(c) Use the policies as guide for determining what data to collect acquire or create; for determining what data management activities to perform, and for creating information systems to perform those activities.

(d) Evaluate either continuously or periodically whether the established policies are being followed, and if not, ensuring that they are followed.

6.9 Conclusion

Data planning and policy making should always be considered as the starting point of all data management activities. This is the reason for explaining data planning and policy-making very early in this course, and ahead of other activities in the data management cycle. Data cost money and other resources to collect, store, protect, communicate and process, and there is no point in spending scarce resources on useless data.

6.10 Summary

In this unit, you have learned about some important aspects of data planning and policy-making. Data planning involves answering questions about why data of different kinds should be collected, stored, processed or communicated to produce information. It also involves answering questions about what data management activities should be performed, how and when the activities should be done, and who should do them.

Data planning and management is interwoven with information management because of the very close relationship between data and information. The increasing necessity for organizations and information systems to acquire and manage data and information efficiently has given rise to a branch of management known as information resource management (IRM). The basic idea of IRM is that information resources are as valuable as money, and hence should be properly and carefully managed by competent information professionals, just as financial resources have been managed by accountants for years.

A data policy is a set of statements that describe the circumstances, objectives and constraints to be followed by people in an organization or information system concerning data management activities. Data policies are usually formulated to ensure that only potentially useful data are created or acquired for processing by an organization or information system. Data policies may be written or unwritten. However, written policies serve as a reference document for ensuring that people in organizations and information systems use standard and consistent rules and methods for performing data management activities.

6.11 Self-assessment exercises

1. Explain the principles of information resource management.
2. In what ways does a data policy manual help an information system to properly manage data?

DATA DEFINITION AND STRUCTURES

	Table of Contents
7.1	Introduction
7.2	Objectives
7.3	Unstructured versus structured data
7.4	Importance of data structure
7.5	Pre-defining the data to be collected
7.6	Guidelines for pre-defining data to be created
7.7	Entities, data records and data fields
7.8	Conclusion
7.9	Summary
7.10	Self-assessment exercises

7.1 Introduction

In Unit 1, data were described as the symbols that have been used to describe something - a person, object, activity, idea, etc. For example, if an animal is described with the symbol's 'peacock', then that are data. Similarly, an idea may be described with the data 'brilliant'.

Persons, objects, activities, ideas, etc., are all examples of entities. Invariably, people describe entities in terms of their attributes. For example, to describe a student, one might describe such attributes of the students as the name, age, sex, etc., with the data 'Tinu Owambe', '23 years', 'Female', etc. are attributes.

You already know that data may comprise alphabetical, numerical, pictorial and other symbols. Moreover, the different symbols can also be combined and arranged in different ways depending upon the purpose for which the data is intended. For instance, the names of students can be arranged in the order of when they registered for a course, or in the alphabetical order of their names.

In this unit you will learn about how data can be planned even before they are actually created. You will also learn how the data to be created can be specified beforehand, how the data that have been created may be sub- divided to meaningful portions and categories.

By understanding the principles of how data can be predefined or grouped into meaningful categories, you will be better able to appreciate how data can, and are often manipulated or processed by men and machines for different purposes.

7.2 Objectives

After studying this unit, you should be able to:

1. Describe the differences between structured and unstructured data.
2. Explain how data are pre-defined before being created or collected;
3. Explain the different ways in which data can be subdivided into separately meaningful portions for ease of understanding and manipulation.

7.3 Unstructured versus structured data

One very important characteristic of data is whether the data are structured or unstructured. Structured data are data that have been uniformly or logically defined and arranged to facilitate human and machine processing and understanding. On the other hand, unstructured data are those that have not been so defined and arranged.

Suppose for instance that you are a clerk in an office who has been given the task of going through the letters of applicants for a job in the office. You are looking for information about the ages of the applicants. It is most likely that you may have to read most of each letter before you get the information you need. The reason is that you will not be sure where exactly in each letter the required information has been written.

Furthermore, suppose that two of the applicants wrote the letters shown in Table 7.1.

Table 7.1: Unstructured data

Amina's application letter

I am Miss Amina Okafor, and I was born 23 years ago in Obolo-Afor village, Imo State. I attended the XYZ College, Kano, and passed the London GCE 'O' level examination in 1988. 1 had credits in English, Economics, Biology, Mathematics and Biology.

John's Application letter:

My name is A. John. I attended ABC Grammar School in Lagos State, from 1983 to 1988. I sat the for the School Certificate examination in June 1995 and passed with credits in eight subjects including English and Mathematics. I am 22 years of age, and male.

The data in the two letters are unstructured because although each applicant provided personal data on such attributes as name, sex, age, school attended, examination and number of subjects passed, the data are not similarly defined or sequenced in the two letters. For example, whereas Amina provided her names in full, John only provided his last name in full. Also, Amina indicated her sex by preceding her name with the data 'Miss', but John indicated his sex last, and with the data 'male'. Finally, whereas Amina listed all the subjects that she passed, John did not. The reason for this, of course, is that the applicants were only asked to write application letters, but were not told how exactly to write them. Hence, the applicants used different writing styles to create the letters.

One method of bringing some structure to the data in Table 7.1 would be, as is often done, to arrange the data in rows and columns as shown in Table 7.2. Data so arranged are structured data in the sense that they have been separated into meaningful components and uniformly sequenced. Notice how, with structured data, one can easily identify the attributes of the entities on which data have been defined.

However, one has to do some work to extract the data from the application letters in order to create Table 7.2. This is the reason why many offices usually ask applicants to fill pre-designed application forms instead of writing application letters. Hence, the form in Table 7.3 might be given to applicants to fill. The form ensures that applicants follow the same order and style in providing their data.

Table 7.2: Structured data

Name	Age	Sex	Exam	Credits
Amina	23	Female	GCE	5
Okafor	22	Male	SSSE	8
P. John				

Finally, you will notice that you will get more or less the same information about Amina when you read the data in either Table 7.1, Table 7.2 or Table

7.3. In order words, different forms of data for presenting the same information.

Table 7.3: Completed application form

Job Application Form A10

Name (Surname Last): Amina Tanko	Sex: Female
Name of Examination: SSSCE	No of credits: S
School attended: XYZ College, Kano	From: 1984 To: 1989

You should now be able to do the following exercises:

Exercise 7.1:

Get hold of an old letter and extract data from the letter under appropriate headings as has been done in Table 7.2.

Exercise 7.2:

Assume that you are a clerk in an office. Design a register to be filled by visitors as they visit your office.

7.4 Importance of data structure

You learned in the previous section that data can be structured or unstructured. Moreover, the same data can often be structured in more than one way as you must have found out when you did Exercises 7.1 and 7.2.

The structure of data is important in two main ways. When you are reading just one application letter, you will be interested only in the structure of the content of the letter. That is, you will be interested in whether the correct words have been used, whether the sentences are grammatically correct, whether the paragraphs are well sequenced, and whether the words, sentences and paragraphs make sense. In other words, one invariably worries about the structure of data when one writes, and also when one reads and interprets data. Data that are logically structured are more likely to convey better information than data that are not logically structured. Hence, data structure should interest you at all times and more so because you are taking a course in data management.

Your English language teacher in high school must have emphasized the importance of structure when you write an essay, or when you read a passage in order to comprehend it. Hence, your teacher probably told you that an essay should have the following structure:

Title
Introduction
Body
Paragraph 1: focusing on first topic or point
Paragraph 2: focusing on a second topic or point

,,,

,,,

Conclusion Summary

> **Exercise 7.3:**
>
> Examine the structure of this unit of your course that you are now studying. Explain what you find in terms of the way the content has been structured. Is the structure helpful? Why or why not'?

Moreover, as you found out in the previous section, we also worry about the structure of data when we create a form to be filled by applicants for a job, or when we create a register for recording data about sales in a shop, or when we create a register for visitors to an office. In each of these instances, we are expecting to record a lot of data about applicants, sales or visitors, and our concern is to make sure that the data about the applicants, sales or visitors are recorded in the same way. When data are so arranged, it becomes a lot easier to find data on a particular applicant, sale or visitor whenever necessary.

7.5 Pre-defining the data to be collected

In Exercise 7.2, you prepared a register to be filled by visitors when they visit the office. In the exercise you were concerned with obtaining the same set of data from each visitor, so you probably ruled columns and lines in a note book or on a sheet of paper. You must have also written headings for the columns. Your register might have looked like Table 7.4

Table 7.4: Register for Visitors

Date	Name of Visitor	Person visited	Purpose	Time in	Time out	sign

You will notice that by using the method in Table 7.4, you have decided, even before visitors start arriving, that:

(a) That each visitor will be required to provide and record seven pieces of data on each visit: (1) the date of the visit, (2) name of the visitor,

(3) person visited, (4) purpose of the visit, (5) time the visitor arrived

(6) time the visitor left, and (7) signature of the visitor.

(b) That visitors will be provided more space to record their names than to write the date of visit, hence, the column widths are different (see Table 7.4);

(c) That visitors are expected to write alphabetical characters in the columns for Name of visitor, Person visited, and Purpose;

(d) That visitors are expected to write sequence of characters that look like a date, such as '12/12/02' or '12-12-2002' in the column for Date;

(e) That visitors are expected to write characters that read like a time, such as '10.43' or '3.10 pm' in the column for Time in and Time out;

(f) That visitors are expected to write characters that looks like a signature in the column for Sign.

In other words, you have pre-defined some aspects of the data to be created by visitors, or, put another way, to be collected by your office. In a nutshell, you have specified

(a) The names or labels of the data to be created or collected (by column headings);

(b) The types of data to be supplied, whether alphabetical (also known as text), numerical, date, time, or image data;

(c) The amount of space to be occupied by the data (by column widths).

You will now be able to appreciate the reason why people design registers for recording data, why people design forms to be filled by people, and why people design questionnaires for people to complete in a research study.

7.6 Guidelines for pre-defining data to be created/collected

Now that you have understood why registers, questionnaires and various types of forms are designed, you should also know some basic rules for pre- defining the data to be collected through a form, a register or a questionnaire:

These are

(i) Make sure you understand the reason why data are being collected. Usually, the reason is in order to subsequently store and process the data to produce information or other data. So, you should know the types of information to be produced, and the types of data required to produce the information. Don't forget, as you learned in Unit 6, that the natures of the data to be created or collected, as well as the information to be produced are usually guided by the information policies of the system or organization for which data are to be collected.

(iii) List all the pieces of data to be created or collected, such as name, address, birth date, etc. List only the data pieces you will need, no more no less. If you fail to list a needed piece of data, data on it will not be collected and available on it. On the other hand, you will be wasting your and other people's time and resources if you list pieces of data that will never be needed. Mind your data require time and money to create, store and process. So, think carefully.

(iii) Provide adequate space for recording each of the listed pieces of data, either in a register, form or questionnaire.

(iv) Provide guidelines to ensure that all those from whom data are to be collected provide data in the same way. For instance, in a form, you might provide the following instruction under the space for name: (Surname first). Another example is to write 'Day, Month, Year) under the space for Birth date on the form.

Exercise 7.4:

Using the above guidelines, design a form to be completed by all applicants for membership in a social club.

7.7 Entities, data records and data fields

You will recall from the first section of this unit that a class of persons, objects or activities e.g., is often referred to as an entity. Hence, visitors to an office, applicants for a job, books in a library, festivals in a village, are examples of entities.

People describe entities in terms of their attributes, thereby creating data. For example, to describe a book (which is a member of the entity books), one might describe such attributes of the book as the title, author's name, publisher, year of publication, etc., and with such data as 'ABC of Home Economics', P. K. Johnson, ABJ Publishers, 1966.

Usually, the set of data that describe each member of an entity, for example, ABC of Home Economics', P.K. Johnson, ABJ Publishers, 1966, is referred to as a data record. In other words, the data on each member of an entity is a record (of data) on the member.

Furthermore, each separately meaningful piece of a record, such as 'ABC of Home Economics' is often referred to as a data element or a data field. In other words, the data record of the book above has four data elements or data fields.

To further illustrate these concepts, let us look at Table 7.5

Table 7.5: Catalogue of books in a library

Author	Title	Publishers	Year	Subject
P.K. Johnson	ABC of Gourmet Cooking	ABJ Publishers	1966	Home economics
J.J. Anderson	Mirror in the sun	ABC Publishers	1970	Fiction
M.A. Tiamiyu	Organization of data in information systems	Infoman Consult	1998	Data management
,,,	,,,	,,,	,,,	,,,

When data are organized in the form of tables as shown in Table 7.5, each row of data is a record on a book. Hence, three records are shown in the table. Also, each column of the table contain data on the same piece of each record, i.e., the first column contains data on authors; the second column contains data on titles, etc. Each column of data in each record is referred to as data element or data field of the record.

> **Exercise 7'5:**
>
> A teacher sets the following question in an examination:
>
> Question: "Describe the human body under the following subheadings - head, trunk, arms and legs, five, senses, the skin, openings i n the body. your answer should have an introduction and a conclusion, and each section should contain no more than 100 words.
>
> Diagrams should he provided"
>
> Using the knowledge that you have gained from this unit, explain what the teacher is trying to achieve by the instructions in the question.

7.8 Conclusion

You should be clear in your mind now that unstructured data are usually more difficult to read and understand by humans than structured data. As you will learn later on in this course, even computers work faster on structured data than on unstructured data. The reason is that unstructured data have no uniform form, sequence or patterns; hence one cannot use a standard method to quickly know where certain data would be in the unstructured mass of data. On the other hand, when data are structured in a table, register or form, it becomes very easy to know or predict where certain pieces or chunks of data will be in the structured data.

7.9 Summary

In this unit, you have learnt about the importance of pre-defining what data to create and collect. Data are created when people write story books, or when students answer questions in an examination.

Good authors are those who are able to structure their story very well. Similarly, you stand a better chance of obtaining high marks in an examination when you plan and structure your answers and points before and while writing them.

People also create or collect data when they complete registers, or fill forms, or questionnaires. They also usually pre-define the data that they want to create or collect by designing registers, forms and questionnaires so that only certain data are created or collected, and so that the data are created in a uniform manner. Hence, data structure is important both when we are writing and reading an essay or book, as well as when we are arranging data in a table, form or register.

In order to define what and how data should be collected, you need, firstly, to determine what information will be required from the data. Secondly, you need to determine the different entities on which data will be collected. Thirdly, you need to list the pieces of data (known as data elements or data fields) to be collected on each member of each entity. Entities include persons, objects, activities, ideas, transactions, etc. Fourthly, you need to specify the names or labels of the data elements or data fields (e.g., Birth date, Sex, Address, etc). Fifthly, you should specify the type of data (eg., alphabetical, numeric, image, etc) that should be created or collected for each data field. Finally, you should specify the amount of space to be provided for recording the data either in a register, a form, or a questionnaire.

7.10 Self-assessment exercises

1. Explain each of the following: data, entity, data record, data field.
2. Use an example to explain the difference between structured and unstructured data.

DATA ARRANGEMENT, GROUPING AND MODELING

Table of Contents	
8.1	Introduction
8.2	Objectives
8.3	Re-arranging data
8.4	Data modeling and data models
8.5	Types of data models
8.6	Hierarchical data structures/models
8.7	Network data structures/models
8.8	Conclusion
8.9	Summary.
8.10	Self-assessment exercises
8.11	Tutor marked Assessments

8.1 Introduction

In the previous unit you learned about the importance of pre-defining the data to be created or collected. You also learned about how people design forms, registers, questionnaires and other forms for ensuring that there is uniformity in the way that data are created or collected. You also learned that it is easier to read and understand structured data than unstructured data because one can use the uniform patterns in the structured data to predict where certain data are likely to be in structured data.

In this unit we will explore further, other approaches to defining, arranging and structuring data for ease of interpretation and understanding. You will learn about the concept of a data model. You will also learn how data models are used in everyday contexts to organize data for human understanding, as well as for machine processing.

8.2 Objectives

After studying this unit, you should be able to:

1. Arrange data using different orders of sorting.
2. Describe a data model, and its purposes.
3. Explain the hierarchical and network modes of arranging data.
4. Arrange data using different sorting modes.
5. Arrange data in either the hierarchical or network modes.

8.3 Re-arranging data

In the last unit we noted that data are symbols that have been used to describe one or more entities. The data could be just one word, say 'elephant', or a set of words or numbers, such as 'An elephant is a very big animal, indeed the biggest land animal. It has tusks, and eats grasses. You also learned that data can also be defined, created and collected in separately meaningful portions. In particular, you learned how data are sometimes organized into data tables, data records and data fields.

Let us now look more closely at one such data (Table 7.4), which shows the sales of medicines recorded in a register by a sales clerk (Table 7.4). The data are provided as records and fields. How many data records and data fields are there? There are eight records and six fields respectively.

Table 7.4: Medicine sales register

Date	Purchaser	Product	Quantity	Price	Value
03/04/02	K. Ahmed	Panadol	50	3.00	150.00
03/04/02	J. John	Aspirin	10	12.00	120.00
04/04/02	P. Uche	MIM Capsules	1	650.00	650.00
04/04/02	A. Zabu	Ace Shampoo	1	300.00	300.00
04/04/02	A. Aina	Cough syrup	1	250.00	250.00
05/05/02	T. Akpan	MIM Capsules	1	650.00	650.00

05/05/02	M. Johnson	Ampicillin	2	125.00	250.00
05/05/02	1). Yusuf	I'ZT Ampules	10	500.00	5,000.00

You will observe that the data in the table are in the natural time order, that is, in the order in which the purchases were made, and in which the data were created.

However, we might want to re-order the records in several other ways as follows:

(a) By the reverse order of the date on which the purchase was made, i.e., the reverse of the natural time order.

(b) By the numerical order of the price of the product, or of the quantity purchased, or of the value of the purchase. The numerical order could also be ascending or descending.

(c) By the alphabetical order of the surnames of the purchasers, or by the alphabetical order of the product names. The order could also be in ascending (ie. from a to z) or descending (ie., from z to a). Table 7.5 shows the same records arranged in the ascending order o the names of the purchasers.

(d) By portions of data, such as the initials of the purchasers, or the month of the sale.

Let us now compare the data in Tables 7.5 and 7.5. In table 7.4, we note that the data record for K. Ahmed's purchase is just before the record or J. John's purchase. This is simply because the two purchases occurred next to each other in time. However, in the re-arranged records in Table 7.5, the two records are now further apart. Although, we have the same set of records, their positions in the table have changed. Similarly, re-arranging the data in the reverse time order or in the numerical order of quantities, prices and values of the purchases will give a different arrangement of the records. In order words, data can often be manipulated and re-arranged in an order that suits our purpose. This is another way of saying that data can often be structured or re-arranged for different purposes.

Table 7.5: Medicine sales register re-arranged

Date	Purchaser	Product	Quantity	Price	Value
03/04/02	K. Ahmed	Panadol	50	3.00	150.00
04/04/02.	A. Aina	Cough syrup	1	250.00	250.00
05/05/02	T. Akpan	MINI Capsules	1	650.00	650.00
03/04/02	.1. John	Aspirin	10	12.00	120.00
05/05/02	M. Johnson	Ampicillin	2	125.00	250.00
04/04/02	P. Uche	MIM Capsules	1	650.00	650.00
05/05/02	D. Yusuf	TZT Ampules	10	500.00	5,000.00

04/04/02   A. Zabu   Ace   1   300.00   300.00
                        Shampoo

The alphabetical and numerical orders of arranging data records are well known by literate people. Hence, words in dictionaries are usually arranged in alphabetical order, and so also are the words in a book index. Library catalogues are also often arranged in the alphabetical order of titles or subjects of the books in the library, and so on. Such alphabetical arrangement of data or of data records often aids human understanding of the data or records. Hence, the following arrangement of the names of seven cities, such as: Abuja, Accra, Berlin, Lagos, London, New York, etc.

Will be more logical, alphabetically speaking, than an arrangement like the following:

Accra, New York, Abuja, Berlin, Lagos, London.

Although the latter arrangement might be useful for some purpose, the purpose is not clear. Is it clear to you? Now when you encounter such an arrangement you probably will initially try to understand why the data are arranged in that way. However, if you cannot understand, you become less sure about what meaning the person who arranged the names of the cities wanted you to obtain from such an unusual arrangement.

Imagine also a dictionary in which the words are not arranged alphabetically. Of course, because there will be no alphabetical order in the sequence of words, it will be extremely laborious to locate specific words in such a dictionary.

Similarly, we often arrange things in numerical or magnitude order, such as, say, from shortest distance to the longest distance, or from oldest person to the youngest person, etc. In order to facilitate human interpretation and understanding it is usually appropriate to arrange quantitative data in either ascending or descending order, unless the data is being arranged deliberately differently. However, in such instances it is always advisable to explain why a different arrangement is being used deliberately so that people would not be confused.

Exercise 8.1:

Explain the criteria that might have been used for arranging the following data:

(a)　12, 34, 16, 45, 100, 203, 344, 2342, 3333

(b)　6, 100, 54, 232, 1, 33...

(c)　Apple, axe, basket, book, box, cat, coffee...

(d)　1, 1.1, 1.1.1, 1.1.2, 1.2, 1.11, 1.2.2, 1.2.3; 2, 2.1, 2.1.1, ...

(e)　Basket, man, toe, baobab, Africa

(f)　A. Thomas, C. David, K. Ahmed, P. Twist, R. Calister...

8.4 Data modeling and data models

An important idea that we stressed in the preceding section is that data can be organized in different ways for different purposes. In order words, data can be structured, arranged or modelled in different ways for different purpose.

A specific arrangement or grouping of data or data records is usually referred to as a 'view' or 'model' of the data, or a data model. Tables 8.1 and 8.2 show two different ways of arranging the records on the sales of the medicines. In other words, they are different 'models' or 'views' of the data records. One might also create different views or models of the data for different purposes. In other words, a data model is the way one might organize the data records in a given situation. It is the method of imposing a meaningful or logical structure on data or records. As noted already, the same set of data may be modelled in different ways for different meaningful purposes.

Suppose now that we have created the following data to describe the different living things:

And non-living things

Father', 'cat', dog', 'house', jackal',
'child', forest', 'owl'

One way to model the data is to arrange them alphabetically. You also probably tried to relate each word to the others as you read through them. But people might disagree on how best to relate the words or data. One person might think and argue that father, cat, dog, house, child - are 'closely' related because they describe things that can be found in a home. However, another person might disagree, arguing instead that the five words should be classified into the following three distinct groups: father, child (because they are human and members of a family); cat, dog (because they are both domestic animals who dislike each other); house (because it is the only non-living object). Furthermore, whereas someone might say that forest, jackal and owl, should be grouped together because both jackal and owl live in forests, another person may argue that dog and jackal should be grouped together because they have similar features. Everyone will probably be partly right, just like the proverbial six blind men who went to 'see' (pardon me, touch) an elephant.

The reason for the differences in the ways that they categorize, classify or group the words (the data) is that they are viewing, structuring or modelling the data in different ways. Each of the different groupings of the data will be appropriate for some occasions and inappropriate for others. In other words, data can often be categorized or modelled differently for different purposes.

8.5 Types of data structures or models

There are two main approaches to grouping or categorizing data or data records in order facilitate human machine processing and understanding. These are the hierarchical, and the network.

8.6 Hierarchical data structures/models

A hierarchical data model is one whereby data records are grouped or interrelated in terms of being super-ordinate or subordinate to one another.

For instance, suppose that we have data on one grandmother, three fathers, two mothers and six children. Let us represent the data on these people as

G1, F1, F2, MI, M2, C1, C2, C3, C4, C5, C6

An obvious way to categorize the data is to group then as follows:

(a) G I
FI,
F2

M1, M2

CI, C2, C3, C4, C5, C6

Suppose however that we know that some of the fathers, mothers and children are related biologically. We can then use this knowledge to structure the data differently as follow

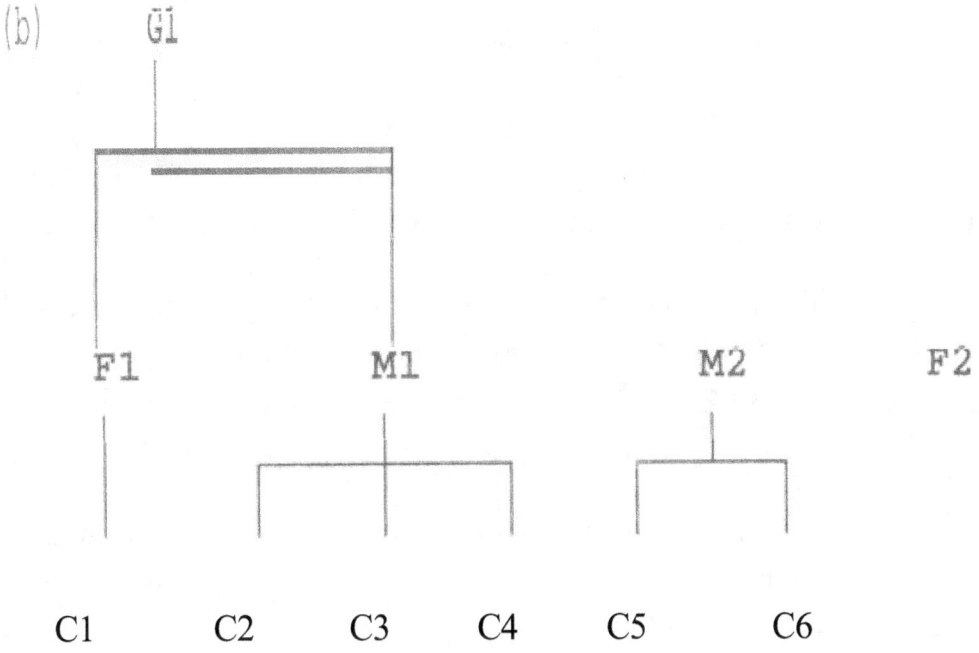

This last grouping and linking of the data records is what is known as the hierarchical method of modelling data. In other words, a parent-child hierarchy is established among the data. Hence, data record G1 is the parent of data records F1 and M1; In turn data record F1 is the parent of data record C1, whereas data record MI is the parent of data records C2, C3, and C4. And so on.

The idea behind linking data or data records in a hierarchy is that, once they are so linked, we can get to the data for a child from the data of the father or mother.

Another everyday example is as follows. We know that there are countries, and within each country states or provinces, and within each state or province, there are towns. Finally, within each town there are streets. So let us assume that we have the following data or data records:

"Nigeria", "Ghana"; "England", "St James's Street"; "Accra"; 'Plot 12", "Ibadan" "London", "High Street"; "Salvation Army Road".

Firstly, we may want to regard each piece of data as separate data in its own right. We can then go on to arrange the data alphabetically, as explained above. However, we can go further to first group them into meaningful or useful categories, and then arrange the data in each category hierarchically from smallest place to largest place, as follows:

Plot 12		
Salvation Army Road	St James's Street	High Street
Ibadan	London	Accra
Nigeria	England	Ghana

Of course, these are how addresses are usually written - from the smallest place to the largest place. In other words, the addresses we often see on envelopes are actually inverse hierarchical arrangements of data, comprising the name of a person, who is living in a particular house, on a particular street, in a particular town, in a particular country, of the world. In fact, data on people and places in the world can be arranged in a huge hierarchy beginning with data on the world, then data on individual countries, then data on cities, towns and villages in the countries, then data on streets in the cities, towns and villages, then data on houses on the streets, and finally data on persons in the houses.

Our second example of hierarchical data structures/models is the way that the content of textbooks is usually structured. The content of (i.e., data in) a textbook is usually arranged in a hierarchy. First of all, we have chapters, under which are sections, and under which are sub-sections, and then paragraphs. Hence, textbooks are usually structured or modelled in a hierarchical way, as shown in Table 8.3.

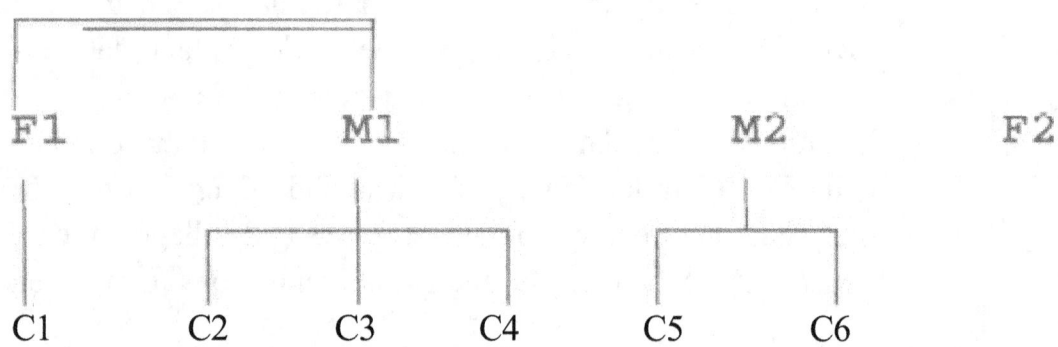

Table 8.3: Hierarchy of Chapters, sections and subsections of a textbook
(Notice also the hierarchical numbering system)

Chapter 1	Section 1.1	Sub-section 1.1.1
		Sub-section 1.1.2
	Section 1.2	Sub-section 1.2.1.
		Sub-section 1.2.2
		Sub-section 1.2.3
		Sub-section 1.2.4
Chapter 2	Section 2.1	Sub-section 2.1.1.
		Sub-section 2.1.2
		Sub-section 2.1.3
	Section 2.2	Sub-section 2.2.1.
		Sub-section 2.2.2
	Section 2.3	Sub-section 2.3.1.
		Sub-section 2.3.2
		Sub-section 2.3.3
...	...	...

Of course, to read the content of sub-section 2.2.1 of the book, you first look for Chapter 2, and then you look for Section 2.2, and then look for Sub- section 2.2.1. In other words, you will be able to locate the data in section

2.2.1 by first going through the data in Chapter 2, and from there through the data in Section 2.2.

Each of the hierarchies that we have explained above looks like a tree. A tree invariably has a trunk, then branches, then leaves. Hence, the hierarchical method of arranging, grouping, linking and modelling data is also known as the 'hierarchical tree' method.

Exercise 8.2

Construct hierarchies between the following data:

Forest, fruits, flower plant, `living things, `mammal, branches, lion, sister, non-living things, brother, kitchen, father, kettle, tree, animal, stone, bed.

8.7 Network data structures/models

This is the second major approach to grouping, classifying and linking data. The network approach is based on the idea that data are, or can be, related in many different ways at the same time. This is to say that data can be grouped, classified or linked in many ways.

A good example of a network is a spider's web. A spider's web look like a basketball or football net, with many links that are joined together at many points. Each of the points in a network where two or more links join up is called a node. In other words, a network will have many links and many nodes. The network approach makes use of the fact that a group of data can often be linked to other groups of data in a sort of network.

An example of a group of data is a data record, which, as you learned in the previous unit, comprises one or more data fields, as shown below:

| Abe Adamu | Male | 27 years | 2 Sokoto St, Ilorin |

Let us now use two previous examples in this unit to illustrate the network approach to grouping, classifying and linking data or data records.

As above, let us consider G1, F1, F2, M1, M2, C1, C2, C3, C4, C5, and C6 represent the data records of one grandmother, two fathers, two mothers, and six children respectively.

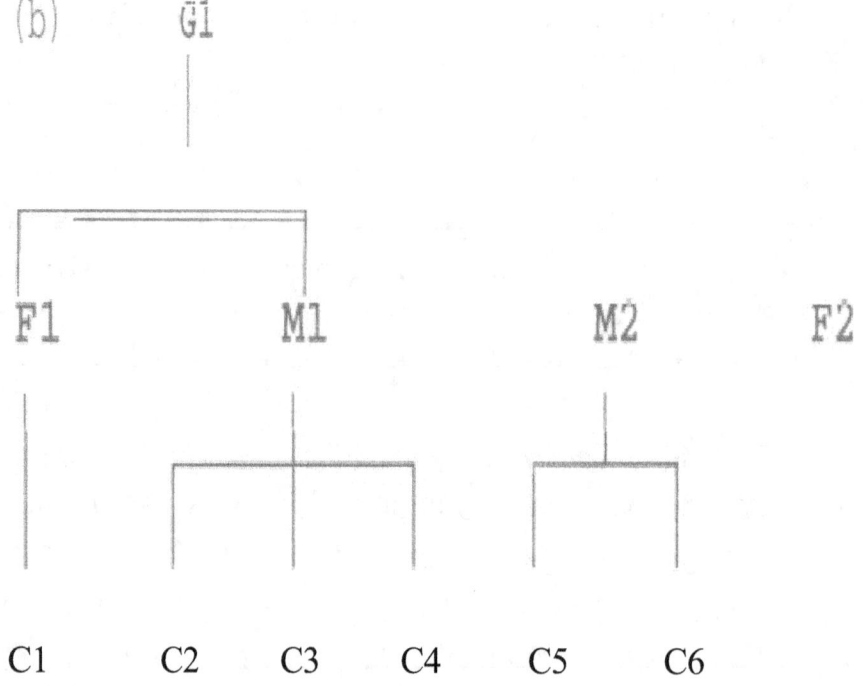

The network approach says that one can often think of many ways in which each data record can be related or linked to the others. Hence, one should also think of other possible relationships between the data records beyond the parent child relationships as in the hierarchical approach. Now let assume that:

- Children C3 and C4 attend the same school;
- Children C1 and C6 are in the same class in different schools;
- Children C3, C5 and C6 are all female;
- Father F2 is the teacher of child C6; fathers F 1 and F2 are friends;
- Mother M 1 and father F2 have the same birth date.

Now let suppose that we want to create linking lines between the data records to reflect the different additional relationships among them. The result of course will be something like as shown in Figure 8.1.

Figure 8.1: Network of data records

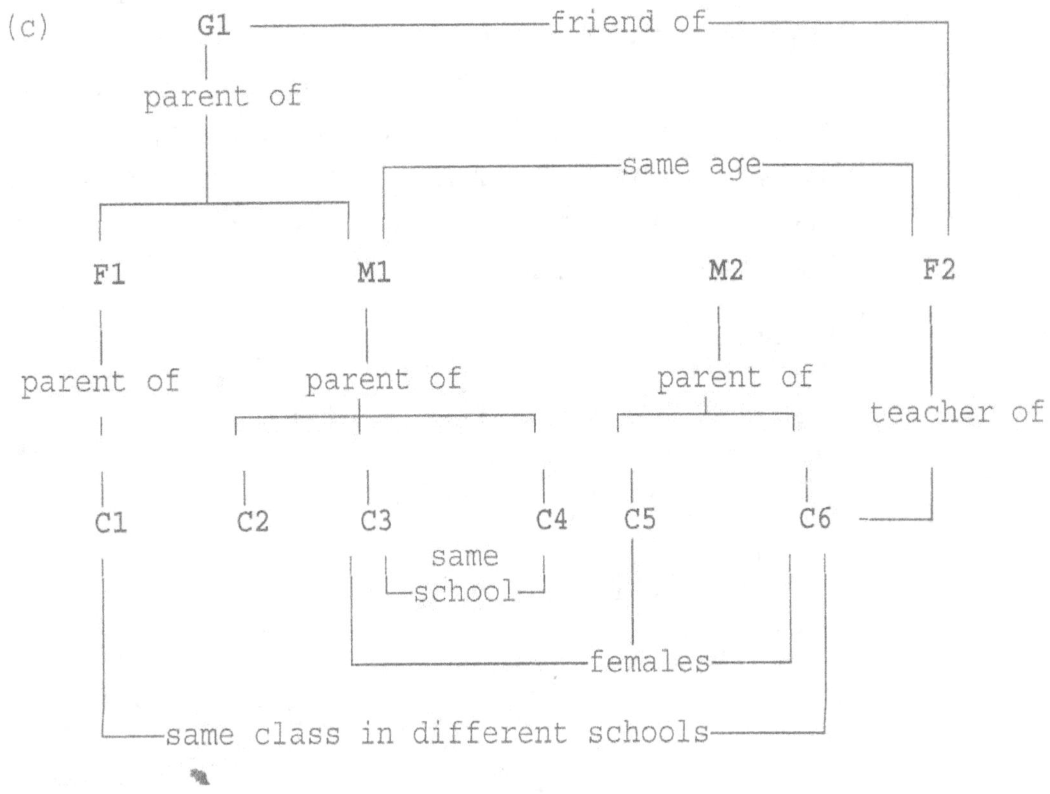

```
(c)           G1 ───────────────── friend of ─────────────┐
              │                                            │
          parent of                                        │
              │                                            │
              │         ┌────────── same age ──────────┐   │
              │         │                              │   │
              │         │                              │   │
             F1         M1                            M2   F2
              │         │                              │   │
              │         │                              │   │
         parent of  parent of                     parent of│
              │         │                              │   teacher of
              │    ┌────┴────┐                    ┌────┴───┐│
              │    │    │    │                    │    │   ││
             C1   C2   C3   C4                   C5   C6 ──┘
              │         │    same                 │    │
              │         └── school ──┘            │    │
              │                                   │    │
              │                    └─── females ──┘    │
              │                                        │
              └──── same class in different schools ───┘
```

You will notice that, as we add more relationships between the data records, the number of links grows, and the network also grows.

You may be wondering why we need to think about such a complex way of thinking about data and data records. The important benefit of the network approach is that it emphasizes that data and data records can often be related, linked or grouped in several ways. Once you appreciate this, you will then be able to think about data not as isolated groups of symbols, but as symbols that often can be linked to other data in different ways. Moreover, you will also then be able to use your knowledge of the potential linkages among data to structure them appropriately for different purposes.

This is similar to the explanation we gave earlier on in this unit on why people might disagree over the most appropriate ways to group, classify or link the following data: father, cat, dog, house, jackal, child, forest, and owl. Actually, there are likely to be many ways to group, classify or link data, and there is really no point trying to say one is better than the other. Rather, one should accept that different groupings, classifications or linkages of data would be more appropriate for different purposes.

> **Exercise 8.3**
>
> Arrange the following set of data on a sheet of paper, and relate then in as many different ways as possible, stating the type of relationship that can possibly exist between each pair of data.
>
> Bed, spoon, kitchen, furniture, knife; dining table, carpet, Jackal', arm chair, TV, bedroom, couch, settee, pressing iron.

8.8 Conclusion

Data can usually be grouped, classified or linked in several ways. One method is to group portions of data into data fields, which, in turn, are grouped into data records. Data can also be arranged or sequenced in different ways for different purposes, including alphabetical, numerical, time order and other types of arrangements. Data are often also arranged in hierarchies, or linked in different ways to form a network of data. All these are different ways of grouping, structuring, classifying, viewing or modeling data. Knowledge of these different approaches to the structuring or modeling of data is important to you in two ways. Firstly, it enables you to structure or model data for different purposes. Secondly, it enables you to quickly understand how the data created or supplied by other people might have been structured.

8.9 Summary

In this unit, you have learned about various ways of structuring or modelling data. Data can be structured as a table of data consisting of rows (data records) and columns (data fields). Data are often initially arranged in natural time order, ie., in the order of the time they were created. But the data can later be re-arranged in other ways, including reverse time order, numerical order, alphabetical order, etc. The alphabetical order of arranging data is frequently used in dictionaries, encyclopedias, book indexes, library catalogues, lists of names, etc.

Data modeling refers to the process of arranging, grouping or linking groups of data for different purposes. The hierarchical approach to data modeling is used to link groups of data in a sort of parent child manner. That is, one group of data may be considered as the parent of another group of data. An example of this is how the contents of textbooks are usually arranged in chapters, sections, subsections, and paragraphs. The network approach to data modeling is used to link groups of data in many ways at the same time.

Knowledge of different approaches to data structuring or modeling is important in data organization and management because it helps us to effectively create and structure data for other people, as well as to effectively interpret the data created or provided by other people.

8.10 Self-assessment exercises

1. Explain the differences between the hierarchical and network approaches to modeling data.

2. Discuss the importance of data structuring or modeling in data organization and management.

3. Enumerate and explain the different methods that can be used to group, arrange, classify and link data.

DATA CAPTURE, ACQUISITION AND COLLECTION

Table of Contents	
9.1	Introduction
9.2	Objectives
9.3	Primary and secondary data Data creation, collection, Data creation
9.4	
9.5	
9.6	Data collection
9.7	Data capture methods and devices Data acquisition
9.8	
9.9	Data collection activities and instruments Conclusion
9.10	Summary
9.11	Self-assessment exercises

9.1 Introduction

In the two preceding units you learned about the overall objectives of data management activities, as well as the policies that are often used by information systems and organizations for creating, acquiring or collecting data. You also learned about how data are often defined and structured before and when they are being created or collected.

In this unit you will learn about the different contexts and methods for creating and acquiring data. Organizations and information systems invariably create data themselves, or capture, collect or acquire the data from their environment. The four verbs, create, capture, collect and acquire, reflect the variety of contexts and processes through which information systems obtain data for subsequent processing, storage and communication to produce information output.

9.2 Objectives

After studying this unit, you should be able to:

1. Distinguish between primary and secondary data.

2. Describe the differences between data creation, collection and acquisition.

3. Explain the importance of the different tasks involved in data collection.

4. Describe and give examples of data collection instruments.
5. Explain data capture and the devices for data capture.

9.3 Primary and secondary data

Information systems creates or acquire primary or secondary data. Primary data are data that are being created or recorded for the first time. For example, a person may be questioned and his answers

recorded as data. However, until recorded the information existed only in the mind of the person being questioned. Data is created only when the answers are recorded in some way. Primary data are data that are being created or recorded for the first time.

Secondary data, on the other hand, are data that someone had previously created, collected, stored or published. Of course the data will have been primary data to the person who created or collected them in the first place. The data will be secondary data to any other person, organization or information system that later acquires the data.

9.4 Data creation, collection, acquisition and capture

Data may be either created, collected, acquired, or captured. These four verbs represent the main ways through which organizations or information systems obtain data as input for their data management activities:

(a) Creation of primary data by or within the organization or system itself,
(b) Collection of primary data from outside the system, usually through the use of various instruments, forms and questionnaires;

(c) Acquisition of secondary data from outside the system, from either paper-based or computerized sources;

(d) Capture of data automatically by a system through various computer input devices such as scanners, cameras, microphones, etc.

9.5 Data creation

Data is created when people write or record data by hand or with devices such as typewriters, keyboards, scanners, cameras, etc. The data may be in the form of long passages of text, numerical data, graphical drawings, or sound.

People create data whenever they write or record symbols such as words and numbers to express some information. The information itself may be derived from other data, or from human precepts or knowledge. For instance, a person may write a summary of a chapter of a book. Of course, the chapter itself consists of data, and the summary is new data created from the original data. New data may also be created by calculating other data - adding, subtracting, graphing, etc. Human precepts, as explained in Unit 1, are things that people experience with any of their five senses - sight, hearing, touch, taste and smell. People sometimes create data to describe what they see, hear, smell, etc. Finally, people also create data to convey part of their knowledge to others.

Natural, scientific and other special languages may be used to create data, as explained in Unit 4. For example, someone may use French language to create data. Another may use a highly technical language to create data. Nevertheless, it is very important that people follow the rules of whatever language they are using to create data so that other people who are literate in the language can easily interpret the data.

9.6 Data collection

Data collection is often undertaken by a system or organization during laboratory or field studies. A laboratory study is done in the laboratory, such as a medical laboratory. Field studies are done by archaeologists or geologists when they dig the ground to discover old civilizations or rocks, by geographers and surveyors when they survey a region, and by social scientists when they interview people or give them questionnaires to complete.

Different data collection methods and instruments are used for data collection. The major methods are direct observation, interviews, and the administration of forms and questionnaires. You have probably used or heard about some of the common instruments that are used by natural scientists and technologists for collecting data in laboratories or workshops, including calipers, scales, thermometers, voltmeters, etc. But there are numerous other more sophisticated instruments. For example, ultrasound equipment is used by medical scientists and technologists to collect data about parts of a human body. X-ray equipment is also used to obtain images of objects. The reason for these instruments is that science and scientists aim for precise ways of measuring and recording data about variables and constants. Hence, more accurate and sophisticated instruments continue to be invented.

The social sciences have been emulating the natural scientists and technologists in this regard. They have also been developing and improving methods and instruments for collecting data on economic, social and psychological variables, such as political attitudes, demand for goods, educational achievement, levels of intelligence, etc. Hence, various standard instruments, scales and tests continue to be developed, including standard forms, questionnaires and examination tests. Table 9.1 shows an example of an instrument (a questionnaire) that a social scientist may use to collect data on the personal characteristics and likeness for different dishes among some respondents (Respondents are persons who answer the questions in a questionnaire).

Table 9.1: An example of a Questionnaire

Dear Respondent,

This questionnaire is designed to collect information about how much you like different types of food. It will take only five minutes of your time, and your answers will be kept confidential. Thank you in advance for answering the questions.

Researcher

A. Bio-data:
1. Age ____ Years 2. Sex (tick one): Male/ Female 3. Tribe_____

B. Preference for local dishes

1. Do you like local dishes (circle one)? Yes No Not sure
2. Do you like foreign dishes (circle one)? Yes No Not sure
3. Do you like local dishes more than foreign dishes? (Circle one)? Yes Not sure

                        Very much   A little   Not at all

Amala and Gbegiri soup	[ ]	[ ]	[ ]
Eba with okro soup	[ ]	[ ]	[ ]
Rice with beans	[ ]	[ ]	[ ]
Salad and dressing	[ ]	[ ]	[ ]
Ogi with akara	[ ]	[ ]	[ ]

9.7 Data capture methods and devices

Data capture is a term often used to refer to the automatic capture and recording of data by mechanical and computer input devices. Examples of computer input devices are scanners, digital cameras, optical character devices, microphones, etc. These devices are usually designed to 'see', 'hear', or 'feel' their immediate environment, and record what they see, hear or feel in the form of data.

For example, imported manufactured products have bar codes. Bar codes are the series of black lines on white background that you find at the back of product packages, particularly imported products. These black lines represent coded information about the nature of the product. A bar code reader (BCR) input device can then be used in a store to collect data about each product as it is sold.

You will also remember that examination candidates are required by WAEC, NECO or JAMB to shade or mark their examination numbers and letters of selected answers on their answer sheets in multiple choice examinations. The purpose of this, if you are not already aware, is to enable WAEC, JAMB and NECO to use optical mark recognition (OMR) data input devices to automatically capture the data (candidates' examination numbers and answers to multiple-choice questions) into computers for computer marking and processing.

9.8 Data acquisition

Data acquisition is usually undertaken to obtain secondary data from various sources. Among the major sources of secondary data are:

(a) Books;
(b) Newspapers;
(c) Technical reports;
(d) Statistical bulletins published by the Federal Office of Statistics, Central and Commercial banks, international organizations, such as the United Nations, etc.;
(e) Annual reports of organizations;
(f) Computer files or databases created by various people, organizations or information systems;

(a) The Internet

An increasingly important source of secondary data is the Internet from which different types of data and information can often be copied or downloaded. Data can also be copied from compact disks (CDs) that have been used to store textual, numeric and image data. Such CDs are referred to as data CDs. Data CDs are physically similar to music CDs, but they contain words, statistics, images and/or sound. Nowadays, books, dictionaries, encyclopedias and statistical data are also being published and sold both as paper-based and CD products.

Exercise 9.2

Browse the website of the **UNESCO** - United Nations Educational, Scientific and Cultural Organization (www.uncsco.org), and download some data and information on scholarships or fellowships.

9.2 Data collection activities and instruments

As explained in section 9.6 above, data collection is often undertaken by a system or organization through laboratory and field studies.

Data collection entails four stages of activities:

(a) Defining what data to collect. This involves deciding the things to be measured, say the weight of some sick children, the temperature of some liquid, the amount of time spent on some jobs, the prices of goods in a market, the performance of students in a subject, etc. Each of the things that we have underlined above can vary depending on the children, liquid, jobs, goods, students, etc. Hence, they are known as variables. In other words, to collect data, one must first determine the variables on which data will be collected. As explained in earlier units of this course, the data to be collected will depend first on the data and information policy of the organization or system, and secondly, on the types of information to be produced with the data.

(b) Selecting or designing the instrument or device to use for collecting the data. An instrument is chosen for measuring the variables if a standard one already exists. Examples of standard instruments are scales, thermometers, tape rules, rain gauges, calipers, etc. However, a new instrument may be designed if no suitable one exists. Remember also that an instrument may be a physical or mechanical device like a thermometer or a scale. But it can also be in the form of a questionnaire or test. For example, questionnaires are usually designed for collecting data from people about their opinions on different issues. Their opinions are the variables, and the questionnaire is the instrument. Also, tests or examinations may also be administered on students to measure their level of knowledge in a subject. Their Level of knowledge is the variable and the test or examination is the instrument.

(c) Using the instrument of device correctly to measure the variables. The instrument that has been chosen or designed for the data collection is used to measure the variable. This is often not as simple as you may think. Using an instrument correctly requires knowledge and experience of the instrument, as well as the variable to be measured. A person who is not experienced in the use of an instrument is unlikely to use the instrument correctly and consistently. This applies to both physical or mechanical instruments as well as questionnaires and tests.

An inexperienced person may measure a distance with a tape rule thrice and still get a different result each time. The question then is which result is the correct one. Similarly, a well-designed questionnaire may be administered very poorly or inconsistently, leading to incorrect or inconsistent data. Also, students may perform poorly in an examination not because the examination is too difficult for their level, but because the examination was conducted in abnormal situations, such as a poorly ventilated examination hall! The result of such an examination may therefore not correctly assess the level of knowledge of different students. In a nutshell, the accuracy or validity of data being collected with an instrument depends on how well the instrument is used to collect the data.

(d) Recording correctly the measurements made with the instrument. Once a measurement is made with an instrument, the measurement must be recorded in some medium as data. The medium may be paper, in the form of laboratory note books, work sheets, registers, etc. The data may also be recorded with computer input devices such as keyboard or scanners. Care needs to be exercised also in the recording process so that recording errors can be avoided.

Exercise 9.4

Design a questionnaire (like the one in Table 9.1) to be used for collecting data from university students about their personal characteristics (e.g., age, sex, religion, etc), study habits (when, where, how, and with whom they study), and attitude to antisocial behavior'(examination malpractices, drug use, cultism; stealing, graffiti, violent protests, etc).

Explain some of the (i) factors that you had to consider, (ii) problems that you encountered, and (iii) decisions you had to make while designing the questionnaire.

9.3 Conclusion

We have deliberately considered data creation, collection, acquisition and capture separately in order to highlight the different contexts and methods through which information systems obtain data for their other data and information management activities. It is nevertheless important to note that data creation, collection, acquisition and capture are interwoven. Data may be created as they are being collected, and data may also be collected or acquired through data capturing devices. Also, a very critical aspect of data creation and acquisition activities is data accuracy. We mentioned data accuracy only briefly during our discussion of the importance of the effective selection, design and use of instruments for measuring and recording data. Don't worry however, as we will be devoting the next unit to this topic.

9.4 Summary

In this unit you have learned about the different processes that organizations and information systems use for acquiring data as input for their other activities. New or primary data are created when symbols are recorded to express or convey information. New data may be captured through various devices. New data are often also created, captured or collected during laboratory or field studies. Finally, secondary data can be acquired from various data or information sources, including books, newspapers, computer databases and the Internet. Various standard instruments for data collection have been designed by natural and social scientists for collecting data, including thermometers, voltmeters, X-ray machines, questionnaires and achievement tests. However, effective and accurate data collection requires careful planning of the data to be collected, careful selection/design and actual use of data collection instruments, and careful recording of the measurements obtained with the instruments.

9.5 Self-assessment exercises

I. Explain the different stages or task involved in a data collection process.

2. Distinguish between primary and secondary data, and how each can be acquired by an information system.

DATA QUALITY CONTROL - FUNDAMENTAL CONCEPTS

Table of Contents

10.1	Introduction
10.2	Objectives
10.3	What is data quality control?
10.4	Accuracy of data
10.5	Validity of data
10.6	Accuracy and reliability of instruments
10.6.1	Accuracy of data collection instruments
10.6.2	Reliability of data collection instruments
10.7	Data collection instruments and procedures
10.8	Conclusion
10.9	Summary
10.10	Self-assessment exercises

10.1 Introduction

Information systems obtain data as input from their environments. Subsequently, the data are processed, stored and communicated to produce information as output from the systems to their environments. In this regard, you may have heard of a very popular saying that 'garbage in, garbage out'. In other words, if an information system obtains bad data as input, it can only be expected to produce bad data or information as output. The saying highlights the importance of processes and techniques for ensuring that the data created or collected by information systems are valid, accurate and reliable.

In the previous unit you learned about the different contexts and approaches to data creation, collection, capture and acquisition. You also learned about the importance of effective design and use of accurate instruments for data collection. In this and the next unit you will learn about various concepts and techniques for enhancing the quality of the data created or obtained by organizations and information systems.

Accordingly, this unit introduces to you the fundamental concepts that should guide the processes within information systems for ensuring the quality of data. For instance, what does data quality control mean? What do we mean by valid, accurate and reliable data?

10.2 Objectives

1. After studying this unit, you should be able to:
2. Explain the importance of data quality control.
3. Distinguish between the accuracy, validity and reliability of data.
4. Distinguish between the accuracy and reliability of data collection instruments.
5. Explain the importance of instruments and procedures in data quality control.

10.3 What is data quality control?

Data quality control refers to the processes and methods by which the accuracy, validity and reliability of data is ensured at the different stages of the data management cycle. (The data management cycle was first explained in Unit 2). The aim of data quality control is to ensure that the data that are created or collected, stored, processed, communicated and used by an information system meets the system's minimum standards of quality.

Data quality is usually described or expressed in terms of such variables are accuracy, validity, adequacy, and so on. Hence, data are often described as valid or invalid, accurate or inaccurate, adequate or inadequate, reliable or unreliable, structured or unstructured, etc.

Data quality control aims to ensure that data are accurate, valid and reliable. Each information system will often specify and work toward achieving acceptable standards of data accuracy, validity and reliability. To achieve this, information systems usually use different strategies and methods for ensuring the quality of their data. Three words have so far been used repeatedly - accuracy, validity and reliability. You may now be wondering what these words mean. So let me explain them.

10.4 Accuracy of data

Before I explain the meaning of data accuracy, you should recall from Units 1 and 8 that data are symbols that have been used to describe or express information about one or more entities. Entities could be persons, objects, events, ideas, or even the attributes of the persons, objects, events, ideas, etc. A word 'variable' is often also used to describe an entity that varies from one situation to another, say the marks obtained by different students in a course, or the names of some children.

Similarly, suppose that the temperature of a room at a certain time was actually or truly 25.6° C. Suppose further that an appropriate instrument, a thermometer, was used to measure and record the temperature at the time as '25° C'. The data are inaccurate because they do not describe the true temperature of the room exactly. Again, the data may be considered adequately accurate for some uses, but not for others.

Notice that this last example introduced the idea of an appropriate instrument for measuring and recording data. The reason for this is that the accuracy of data depends, firstly, on the use of an appropriate instrument for measuring and recording data. To illustrate the importance of appropriate and accurate instruments, let us suppose that instead of using a thermometer, a tape rule was used to measure the length, width and depth of the room. Of course, the data will not be temperature data. The data on the length, width and depth of the room may be accurate, but they do not describe or express information about the temperature of the room.

Finally, note that the more accurate data are, the more likely that they will convey the correct information about the entity described by the data. Conversely, the more inaccurate data are, the less likely can correct information be obtained from the data.

10.5 Validity of data

Data validity refers to the extent to which a set of data expresses accurate and true information about an entity. In other words, data validity requires that (i) the data are accurately measured and recorded, and (ii) that the data conveys true information about the entity described by the data.

We will explain the data validity with three examples.

Firstly, suppose that the following data is created to express information about the two persons:

'Abu is older than John'

The data will be considered valid if Abu is actually or truly older than John. Conversely, the data will not be valid if Abu is not actually or truly older than John. In other words, data that expresses untrue information about an entity is invalid as far as that particular entity is concerned.

For the second example, suppose that a person actually eats bean stew once every week. If the person, in response to a question, says 'four times per month', the data may not be valid. This is because 'four times per month' does not convey the same information as 'once per week'. A person who eats beans stew once per week actually eats it regularly once every seven days. However, a person who eats the food four times per month might eat the food on four consecutive days in a month, or in other sequence of four days different from 'once per week'. This second example illustrates the fact that the validity of data decreases as the data becomes less and less accurate.

Finally, a third example that is slightly different from the first two. Suppose we are interested in knowing the weight of a person, but rather than use scale, we use a tape rule to measure the chest span of the person. This is a case of using a wrong instrument or procedure to measure and record data. The data obtained with the tape rule will be a valid description of the chest span of the person if the data were recorded accurately. However, the data is unlikely to be a valid description of the weight of the person, unless we are prepared to accept that data on the chest span of a person correctly describe that person's weight. Data are considered valid only when they express true information about entities. Data will be both valid and accurate if they express true and exact information about entities. However, data may be accurate but invalid, as highlighted in the example above.

This last example highlights the fact that invalid data can result from using a wrong instrument to collect some required data. The wrong instrument will usually measure and collect data different from what are required. Although the wrong instrument might measure such wrong data accurately, the data will be invalid or useless for the intended purpose. Moreover, even when an appropriate instrument is used, inaccurate data can arise from mistakes in using the instrument or in recording the data. Such data will be inaccurate, and can also be rendered invalid if the margin of error is high. The reason is that the more inaccurate the data, the more likely that they will express untrue information about the entity.

The validity of data is important in data management because it tells us whether the data truly describe or express information about an entity. Conversely, any information about an entity obtained from valid data is more likely to be true than information obtained from invalid data.

10.6 Accuracy and reliability of instruments

The discussion in the preceding section highlighted the importance of using appropriate instruments correctly to measure and record data. However, the instrument itself must be accurate and reliable. In other words, an instrument must, when used correctly, be able to do what had been designed to do accurately and reliably.

10.6.1 Accuracy of data collection instruments

A data collection instrument is considered accurate if it can be used to measure a variable with little or no error. Suppose that the true weight of a truck is 2.34 tons. A new weighing instrument will be considered accurate if it reports the weight of the truck exactly or with negligible error. In order to determine the accuracy of the new instrument, the true weight would have been established previously using a well-tested or standard instrument or method. Similarly, a new questionnaire might be subjected to an accuracy test by using it to collect data that is already known. For instance, a question in a questionnaire might be used to ask for the date of birth of some students, although their dates of birth have been obtained from other sources. That question (which can be considered as a sub instrument of the questionnaire instrument) will be considered a highly accurate instrument if the dates supplied by the students in response to the question are exactly the same as, or very close, to their true dates of birth.

10.6.2 Reliability of data collection instruments

A data collection instrument will be considered reliable if it reports the same data every time it is used to mention the same thing. Hence, the new weighing instrument measure in the above example will be considered reliable if it reports a weight of exactly or very close to 2.34 tons for the truck each and every time it is used.

You will recall from the previous unit that instruments for measuring and recording data include not only physical or mechanical instruments such as tape rules, weight scales and voltmeters, but also social survey questionnaires and educational achievement tests. In other words, questionnaires and tests can also be described as accurate/inaccurate and/or reliable/unreliable. Hence, a question in a questionnaire that asks respondents about when they usually wake up in the morning will be considered to be a very reliable instrument if each respondent provides the same time waking time each and every time the question is asked. Also, a whole questionnaire will be considered to be highly reliable if more or less the same data can be collected with the questionnaire each time it is used. Finally, an examination test in a subject will be considered to be a reliable instrument for determining the achievement of students in that subject only if the student's performance will be more or less be the same if they do the test on two or more occasions.

10.7 Data collection instruments and procedures

The qualities of data are affected by the quality of the instruments that are used to measure, record or create data. Secondly, a good instrument used in a wrong manner often also leads to data of low quality. Thirdly, low data quality can result from errors made in recording the data that has been measured with a good instrument. Finally, errors can also arise when data are copied or transferred from one medium (say, paper) to another medium (say, paper or computer). In other words, quality instruments and procedures are required to ensure that quality data are created or collected.

Let us now examine the desirable attributes of a quality instrument. A good instrument for collecting data on an entity is an instrument:

(a) That is accepted by experts in a discipline or profession as the standard instrument collecting valid data on the entity; or

(b) That, although not yet considered standard, had previously been used by different people to obtain valid data on the entity; or

(c) That experts agree will collect valid data on the entity when used; or

(d) That has been tested to be accurate and reliable.

Moreover, in order to ensure that a good instrument is used correctly, the procedure for using the instrument to measure and record data should be:

(i) Should be specified as a sequence of tasks that can be easily understood and performed;

(ii) consistent each and every time that the instrument is used;

(iii) Written so that people who want to use the instrument can confirm the steps of the procedure.

Exercise 10.1

Answer True or False, (circle one):

(a) The validity of data depends on accuracy of data. [True/False]

(b) Data considered inaccurate for a purpose may still be considered accurate for another purpose. [True/False]

(c) The ability of a person to describe an entity is a data collection instrument. [True/False]

(d) Reliability of depends on reliability of the instrument used. [True/False]

(e) Using a wrong instrument to collect data on an entity can yield valid data. [True/False]

(f) The procedure and process of interviewing a person is not a data collection instrument. [True/False]

(g) Using a wrong instrument to collect data on an entity can yield reliable data. [True/False]

Slightly inaccurate data may be considered valid.

(h) Validity of data depends on data collection instrument. [True/False] Using a wrong instrument to collect data on an entity can yield accurate data.

(i) [True/False]

10.8 Conclusion

In a nutshell, the objective of data quality control is to improve the quality of the data collected by information systems. This is achieved by implementing strategies to ensure that the data are valid, accurate and reliable. Among the strategies is to ensure that the instruments used for collecting data are accurate and reliable. Other strategies are to ensure that the correct procedure for using the instruments is explained and consistently used, and that the measurements made with the instruments are correctly recorded as data. Data quality control is required at all stages of the data management cycle, but especially when data are being created, collected or acquired by an information system.

10.9 Summary

In this unit you have learned about the processes of data quality control. These are the processes used by information systems to ensure that the data that they create or collect, process, store, communicate and produce are valid, accurate and reliable. Valid data are data that express true information about an entity. Accurate data are data that describe or express true information about an entity very precisely or exactly. Hence, data quality control aims for data that express both true and exact information about entities.

Data quality depends on the quality of data collection instruments and the procedures for using the instrument to measure and record data. A good instrument should be both accurate and reliable. An instrument is accurate if it collects data on an entity with very little or no error. A reliable instrument will collect the same data if repeatedly used to collect data on the same entity. The accuracy and reliability of instruments also depends on how they are used to collect data. Hence, data quality control aims to ensure that both quality instruments and procedures are used to create and collect data for information system.

10.10 Self-assessment exercises

1. 'A standard instrument such as a tape rule can sometimes yield invalid data'. Explain.

2. Answer true or false:
   (i) Valid data convey true information about an entity. [True/False]
   (ii) The end result of using a good instrument may be invalid data. [True/False]
   (iii) Accurate data always convey true information about an entity. [True/False]
   (iv) High accuracy is required to assure high validity. [True/False]
   (v) Data measured with a reliable instrument or method will also be reliable. [True/False]
   (vi) An accurate instrument will also be a reliable instrument. [True/False]
   (vii) A standard instrument for measuring an entity can yield invalid data. [True/False]
   (viii) An reliable instrument may still yield invalid data. [True/False]
   (ix) Data collection instruments must be tested for validity, accuracy and reliability. [True/False]
   (x) Data measured with a reliable instrument will be accurate. [True/False]

Data quality control - context and strategies

Table of Contents		
11.1	Introduction
11.2	Objectives
11.3	Planning of data quality control
11.4	Data quality control before, during and after
11.5	Data quality control before data are collected
11.6	Data quality control during data collection
11.7	Data quality control after data are collected
11.8	Data quality control by humans and machines
11.9	Conclusion
11.10	Summary
11.11	Self-assessment exercises

11.1 Introduction

In Unit 10 you learned about important data quality control concepts such as data validity and accuracy, and the accuracy and reliability of data collection instruments. You also learned that both accurate and reliable instruments, as well as the consistent use of appropriate procedures for using the instruments are required to ensure the collection of data of good quality.

In this unit you will learn more about data quality control. However, the emphasis here will be on the different contexts, processes and strategies of data quality control. Data are created and used to express and obtain information in all aspects of human endeavor. People understand that information is best conveyed with good quality data, and also that good information can only be obtained from good quality data. Hence, different data quality control strategies have been developed over time by different disciplines, professions, organizations and information systems to ensure high data quality.

Accordingly, the aim of this unit is to enable you to learn about the diversity of data quality control contexts and strategies. In this regard, the concepts of data accuracy, validity and reliability that you learned in Unit 10 will assist your understanding of the common rationale underlying the strategies for data quality control in different contexts.

11.2 Objective

After studying this unit, you should be able to:

1. Explain the tasks involved in planning for data quality control.
2. Explain the different data quality control contexts and strategies.
3. Explain the methods that can be used for data quality control in laboratories research.
4. Contrast human and computerized approaches to data quality control.

11.3 Planning of data quality control

In the previous unit you learned that data quality control is the process by which the accuracy, validity and reliability of data is ensured at the different stages of the data management cycle. The aim of data quality control is to ensure that the data that are created or collected, stored and processed by an information system meets that system's minimum standards of quality. Data quality control is required at all stages of the data management cycle, but especially when data are being created, collected or acquired by an organization or information system.

The process of data quality control should always be planned and carefully implemented to ensure maximum effectiveness. The process should begin before data are actually collected. Three main tasks are involved when planning for data quality control, as follows:

(a) Establishing data quality policies and standards: You will recall that Unit 6 - Data Planning and Policy Making explained the nature and importance of data planning and policies as guide for data management activities. Data quality control should start right from when organizations and information systems are planning their data requirements and policies. In this regard, a very important task is to establish the minimum standards of quality that the data collected by the information system should meet. As you learned in the previous unit, data validity cannot be compromised. But data accuracy can be set high or low depending on the uses for which the data will be put. Of course, even data accuracy cannot be compromised too far, else the data will be so inaccurate as to be invalid and useless.

(b) Adopting or developing the language to be used for creating and recording the data. Remember that data are the symbols that have been used to describe or express information about entities. You will also recall from Unit 4 - Languages for Data Organization that the symbols used for creating data are invariably selected from human or special languages. Hence, a second important task in planning for data quality control is to select or design a language to be used for recording the data. Although natural languages are usually used, information systems sometimes develop special languages whose symbols and rules are then used to create data.

(c) Developing data collection instruments and procedures. Finally, you also learned in the previous unit that data collection instruments and procedures must be planned, designed and tested in order to ensure that the data collected with the instruments and procedures are of adequate quality. Accordingly, the third important task in planning for data quality control is to select or develop quality data collection instruments and procedures.

11.4 Data quality control before, during and after

Data quality control can be performed before, during and after data are collected. As explained above, one of the main tasks in planning for data collection is to design effective data collection instruments and procedures. Data quality can be controlled before data are actually collected by implementing strategies for producing valid, accurate and reliable data collection instruments and procedures. Planned and pre-tested instruments and procedures are more likely to generate good quality data than unplanned and untested instruments. Strategies for controlling data quality before data are collected are explained in section 11.5.

Data quality can also be controlled during data collection by ensuring that the instruments and procedures are used consistently as had been designed. Good instruments and procedures may still not generate good quality data if not properly used. This is particularly true when humans are required to use the instruments and procedures to collect data. Humans are prone to boredom, inconsistency and error. Different people might use an instrument differently, thereby collecting different and probably incompatible data. Moreover, even the same person might use an instrument differently at different times, thereby also leading to incompatible data. Strategies for controlling data quality during data collection are explained in section 11.6.

Finally, data quality can be controlled after data had been collected by cross checking the data for errors. This can be done by humans and/or machines. Strategies for controlling data quality after data are created or collected are explained in section 11.7.

11.5 Data quality control before data are collected

We explained in the previous unit that a good data collection instrument must be both accurate and reliable. This often requires repeated testing and improvement of an instrument until it meets minimum standards of accuracy and reliability. Manufacturers of mechanical and electronic instruments invariably test each manufactured instrument for accuracy and reliability. And only those that pass their quality control tests are sold to the world.

Designers of questionnaires, instrument and examination tests often also subject them to accuracy, reliability and validity checks. They do this in different ways, including:

(a) Ensuring that there are no confusing, embarrassing or annoying words or questions in each questionnaire or form. Confusing or embarrassing or annoying words or questions can cause respondents to provide false or inaccurate data unknowingly. Annoying questions can cause them to refuse to provide any data.

(b) Asking respondents for the same information with differently worded questions at different points in a questionnaire and finding out whether the data provided are consistent or almost the same. The more similar or consistent the data provided in response to the different questions, the more likely that the data are true, accurate and valid.

(c) Asking the same respondents to answer the same questionnaire at two different occasions, say one month apart, and finding out whether the data provided at the different occasions are consistent or almost the same. The more consistent or similar the data the more reliable is the questionnaire.

(d) Ensuring that examination tests are neither too simple not too difficult for the intended candidates. An examination that is too difficult will be failed by most candidates including many brilliant ones. Hence, the examination will not provide good results or data for separating poor from good candidates. Conversely, an examination that is too easy will be passed by almost every candidate. Hence, the results also cannot be used to separate poor from good candidates. In other words, the results or data from examination questions that are too easy or too difficult will not be expressing true information about the candidates. Hence the data will not be valid.

Questionnaire or test is intended to use their knowledge to determine whether the questionnaire or test is a good one. In other words, experts are asked to take a hard look at the questions in the questionnaire or test to say whether the questions are reasonable and likely to the collection of valid data from respondents or candidates.

Exercise 11.1

This exercise is to improve your appreciation of the importance of language and the wording of questions in questionnaire instruments. Below are four ways in which a question may be asked in a questionnaire:

When do you usually have your breakfast?

What is the most common time you like to take your breakfast?
When do you usually eat your food in the morning?

What time do you consider most appropriate for eating breakfast?

(a) Which question(s) is likely to be confusing? What words in the question are likely to be confusing?

(b) Which question do you like the best?

(c) Write two other questions to ask for the same information.

Exercise 11.2

Ask three of your friends or course mates the following questions and record their answers:

(i) Which do you like most: white rice, jollof rice, fried rice?

(ii) Which colour do you like least: blue, green, purple, grey, can't say?

(iii) How often do you eat eba? Very often, often, seldom, never

(iv) How many hours do you spend watching TV per week? Hours

(v) How many hours do you spend listening to music per week? 0-1 hour, 2-3 hours, 4-S hours, 6-7 hours, 8-9 hours, more than 9 hours

Ask them the same questions again after two weeks. Are their answers the same? Which questions provided the most and least reliable answers. Can you explain why?

11.6 Data quality control during data collection

Data quality can be improved during data collection by using the same instrument to measure an entity twice before recording the measurement as data. For example, a tailor might measure a client's chest span with the same tape rule twice before recording the data.

Another common method for ensuring quality data during data collection is to use more than one instrument to measure and record the same data so that the data collected with different instruments can be used to cross-check one another for accuracy. For example, the temperature of a room could be measured with two different thermometers so that each can serve as a check on the other. Also, a questionnaire and an interview could be used to collect data from the same people so that their answers can be cross-checked with each other.

This method of multiple instruments is also used whenever a panel of judges, instead of only one judge, is asked to decide a criminal case, to decide the most beautiful woman in a contest, or to decide who won each round of a boxing match. For example, in a boxing match, the data required are the number of points scored by each boxer in each round. Three or more judges are often used because a single judge might be biased unknowingly or deliberately. The average of the points recorded by the judges might then be recorded as the authentic, valid data. The logic is that the three or more judges (different instruments) cannot be all biased in the same way at the same time, although, with human beings this sometimes happen.

11.7 Data quality control after data are collected

Textual, numeric and other types of data can usually also be checked for correctness after the data are created or collected. Recall that textual data comprises mostly words, sentences and paragraphs, whereas numeric data comprise mostly of numbers.

(i) Textual data

There are two main methods for cross-checking textual data:

(a) A spelling check of the accuracy of the words in a document can be done either by a human being or more efficiently by computer. Whether done by humans or computer, an appropriate dictionary is provided, against which each word is checked. The dictionary will be the dictionary of the natural or special language that has been approved for creating and recording in the information system.

(b) A check of the grammatical structure of the sentences and paragraphs in the document can be performed to remove any potential ambiguities in the sentences thereby reducing or minimizing misinterpretation of the data.

(ii) Numeric data

For numerical data, checks can be performed to determine whether the values of the data are likely to be inaccurate. For example, suppose that data had been collected and recorded on the ages of students in a secondary school. Of course, any data like '45 years' or '8 years' will be considered to be suspicious, and probably inaccurate and invalid. In other words, for quantitative data, the values of the data are checked to determine if they could have been true. Extremely low and extremely high values are prime candidates for suspicion, and are often subjected to double checking.

(iii) Structured data

You will also recall from Units 7 and 8 that data can be pre-defined or re-structured into separately meaningful portions. An example of such pre-defined data, which you first encountered in Unit 8, is shown as Table 11. 1. You learned in Unit 8 that the data in the table have been structured into the following fields: date, purchaser, product, quantity, price and value.

For such structured data, checking for data accuracy can be done by finding out if the data in, say the date column, are all dates. A date will look like 'DD/MM/YY' or 'DD-MM-YY' where the DD, MM and YY stand for the two digits representing day of month, month of year, and year, respectively. Similarly, the data in the purchaser field are expected to comprise only alphabetical letters (no numbers or special characters are allowed except the full stop or hyphen). Also, each separate surname, first name or initial must begin with a capital letter. These are the rules that the data in the purchaser field must obey. Hence, the data in the field can be checked to find out if any data are violating the rules. Finally, the data in the quantity, price and value fields are all expected to be numbers, so no alphabetical characters are allowed in the field.

In the same way, data that have been entered into registers, forms and data tables can be checked to find out if they violate any rules.

Table 11.1: Medicine sales register

Date	Purchaser	Product	Quantity	Price	Value
03/04/02	K. Ahmed	Panadol	50	3.00	150.00
03/04/02	J. John	Aspirin	10	12.00	120.00
04/04/02	P. Uche	MIM Capsules	1	650.00	650.00
04/04/02	A. Zabu	Ace Shampoo	I	300.00	300.00
04/04/02	A. Aina	Cough syrup	1	250.00	250.00
05/05/02	T. Akpan	MIM Capsules	1	650.00	650.00
05/05/02	M. Johnson	Ampicillin	2	125.00	250.00
05/05/02	D. Yusuf	TZT Ampules	10	500.00	5,000.00

(iv) Data from examinations and questionnaires

The marks obtained by the candidates in an examination may be checked to determine if the marks can be used to assess the candidates' knowledge of a subject. Too many failures or too many passes may indicate that the examination is either too difficult or too easy. In either case, the data will not be too good for assessing the candidates' knowledge. Moreover, the marks obtained by candidates in related subjects (say, mathematics and physics, or mathematics and further mathematics, or English language and English literature) may be used to cross check one another. Similarly, the data collected with a questionnaire can be analyzed to find out if the answers (data) supplied by each respondent to certain questions are consistent with the answers (data) supplied by the respondent to other questions.

11.8 Data quality control by humans and machines

Data quality control checks can be performed by humans and/or machines. Humans usually perform better than computers when complex human knowledge and feelings are required to measure and record data in critical situations, such as when a judge must pronounce an accused person guilty or not guilty to a murder charge. Human judges are also used in data collection situations that although not critical, still require complex human knowledge and emotions, including cooking and beauty contests.

However, machines can usually be programmed to perform many types of data quality control checks. We have explained already that a computer can be programmed to automatically reject data that do not meet certain requirements (e.g., digits or numbers being entered as part of a person's name). Computers can also be programmed to go through massive data to fish out suspicious, and possibly inaccurate, data faster and more accurately than humans. For instance, a computer can read through a 10,000-word computer file within a few seconds to find all the incorrectly spelt words. No human can do that, and most humans will overlook some of the incorrectly spelt words no matter how much time they have to do the work.

11.9 Conclusion

Data quality control is a crucial data management activity because it determines the quality of the data collected and managed by an information system to produce information. Data quality control seeks to ensure that the resources of an information system are not wasted on collecting, storing and processing inaccurate, unreliable or invalid data. Good information can only be obtained from good data; the alternative is clearly 'garbage in, garbage out'. Hence, each organization or information system must implement policies and strategies to ensure the collection and processing of data of adequate quality.

11.10 Summary

In this unit, you have learned more about the data quality control. Effective data quality control demands good planning. Such planning entails three main tasks (i) establishing policies and minimum data quality standards, (ii) developing the language in which data are to be recorded; (iii) and developing accurate and reliable instruments and procedures for measuring and recording data. Other quality control strategies can be used during and after data collection. Multiple instruments or multiple measurements can be used to cross check the accuracy of data being collected. Computers can also be programmed to automatically reject poor quality data as they are being created or collected. Moreover, humans and computers can be used to check through already collected data to find incorrect or suspicious data, such as wrongly spelt words or unreasonably high or low numeric data.

11.11 Self-assessment exercises

1. Explain the importance of data quality control in the data management process.

2. Explain with example why multiple instruments or multiple measurements are sometimes used during data collection.

3. Describe at least three ways in which computers can be used to assist data quality control.

DATA STORAGE MEDIA AND ORGANIZATION

Table of Contents		
12.1	Introduction	
12.2	Objectives	
12.3	Data storage and retrieval	
12.4	Data storage media	
12.5	Data storage in story books and textbooks	
12.6	Data storage in paper forms, registers, etc.	
12.7	Data storage and retrieval in computers	
12.8	Data in computer files and folders	
12.9	Data in computer databases	
12.10	Conclusion	
12.11	Summary	
12.12	Self-assessment exercises	

12.1 Introduction

In the last three units you learned about how data are created or collected by information systems. You also learned about various strategies that information systems use to ensure that data of adequate quality are created or collected.

Information systems usually store the data that they create or collect before or after processing the data to produce information. Information systems need to plan for, and use effective and efficient methods for storing their data. Effective methods are those that achieve their objectives. Efficient methods are those that achieve their objectives at the least cost.

Data storage brings into focus some interrelated issues. The first issue is the dependence of the aims of data storage and data retrieval. In other words, data must be stored in order to achieve the objective of data retrieval. The second issue is the types of media on which data can be stored. Types of media include paper, computer disks and tapes, film, audio and video cassettes, CDs (ie, compact disks), etc. A third issue is how the data are to be organized and stored in each type of media. You learned about this somewhat in Unit 7 - Data definition and structures and in Unit 8 - Data arrangement, grouping and modelling.

In this unit you will learn about these and other issues, and the different strategies that information systems often use to store and retrieve data effectively and efficiently.

12.2 Objectives

After studying this unit, you should be able to:

1. Explain the importance of data storage, and the relationships between data storage and retrieval.
2. Explain the types of media that can be used to store data.
3. Describe how data are organized and stored in different types of paper documents.
4. Explain how data are organized and stored on computer media such as hard disks, diskettes and compact disks.

12.3 Data storage and retrieval

Data storage is never an end in itself. Data must always be stored with a view to subsequent retrieval and use. Clearly, no value can be obtained from the stored data that cannot later be found or retrieved. Hence, a very important problem in data storage is how to store data on each type of media in such manner that the data can later be effectively and efficiently found and retrieved from the media.

You will learn more about data retrieval later on in Units 14 and 15. In the meantime, you should be aware of the fact that data should always be stored with effective data retrieval in mind. Hence, when storing data of any kind in any medium (paper, computer, etc), the emphasis should always be on making sure that the data can be easily located and retrieved. In other words, adequate time, effort and logic should be devoted to data storage so that data retrieval can be very fast. Put in another way, care and time should be spent during data storage so that time can be gained during data retrieval. Conversely, data stored hurriedly may be difficult or impossible to find. Of course, stored data that cannot be found later is of no value because an information system would not be able to use the data to produce information and other data.

12.4 Data storage media

Information systems store data in the following major types of media: human brains, paper, microforms, computer media, and audio and video tapes and CDs.

(i) Human brain

The human brain was used to store data and information long before paper was invented. However, the human brain provides a store not only for data, but also knowledge.

You will recall from Unit 1 that knowledge is the extent of familiarity possessed by a person with certain facts, truths, principles or subjects. Knowledge consists of facts, truths and ideas that fit together to form a coherent and meaningful whole. A person's overall knowledge influences how he perceives the world around him. In other words, knowledge is used by people to interpret and evaluate new information. Knowledge serves as a pool from which people can extract specific truths, facts, ideas for informing or instructing other people. Data are stored in human brains as part of knowledge. Data are also created from a person's knowledge when the person uses symbols to express information extracted from the knowledge.

Nobody knows for sure how data and knowledge are organized and stored in the human brain. Psychologists claim however that human beings store data in either short-term or long-term memory. Data in short term memories are stored for a short time, and are lost unless committed to long term memory. Among the strategies used by people to store data in long term memory is to say, read or write the data repeatedly. Is this not how you commit data to memory? If not, how do you do it? There are of course many other methods which we cannot explain here.

(ii) Paper

Paper became a media for storing data when papyrus was invented. Data were initially stored on paper by writing long hand until printing was invented. Data are still mostly recorded on paper in the form of published or unpublished, as well as printed, typed and hand-written documents. Among the well-known paper-based data and information sources are books, newspapers, journals, technical reports, correspondence, etc.

(iii) Microforms

Microforms is the general word used to describe all miniature but non-computerized storage media such as film rolls, film slides, microfiche, etc. Data are stored in these media as miniature or microscopic images, hence, the name microforms. The data are stored on such media by photographing or scanning pages of paper or computer documents, and then transferring the images unto film rolls, film slides or microfiche. The major advantage of microforms is that they require much less space to store than paper. However, special equipment such as reading glasses or lens, film projectors, microfiche readers, etc, are required to access the data in these media.

(iv) Computer media

Data are increasingly being stored on computer media. Computer media include tapes, disks, diskettes, compact disks (CDs), smart cards, mobile phone recharge cards, etc. Data are stored on computer media as data files. A data file on a computer media is any collection of data stored under a single name. The data might comprise alphabetical, numerical or special characters, or digitized images. (You may review Unit 5 for explanation on how computers store digitized images). The data in the file may also be subdivided into data records and fields, as you learned in Units 7 and 8.

(v) Audio and video media

The gramophone record was a popular media for storing sound data before the arrival of audio and video tapes and CDs. Tapes and CDs are now used for storing sound, image and voice data. You most probably had listened to a Michael Jackson tape or CD before, but tapes and CDs are now used as media for publishing books, dictionaries and encyclopedias. Indeed, some of the study materials in some of your NOU courses might be provided on audio or video tapes or CDs.

Exercise 12.1

Use an audio tape recorder to record the content, of this unit (up to and including this exercise) into a cassette tape. Read aloud, making sure that you pause appropriately at commas, semi-colons and full stops. Separate the sections and the paragraphs with appropriate pauses, as you read along.

The above exercise illustrates how data are recorded unto, and stored on audio and video tapes. We will now explain some of the usual strategies used for effective data storage on two other very common types of storage media: paper and computer media.

12.5 Data storage in story books and textbooks

Data are organized into paper-based books in various ways depending on the type of book. Data in a fiction or story book are usually organized into chapters, but the chapters may not even have titles. A table of contents may also not be provided, and an index is usually not provided. This method of organizing and storing data in such books is adequate because all readers of the book are expected to read the book from the beginning to the end. The assumption is that no reader will be interested in reading only portions of the book, because the story cannot be understood without reading the whole book. However, without tables of content and index, it is usually difficult to locate specific passages, sentences or words from such a book.

By contrast, textbooks invariably have tables of contents, subject and name indexes, glossaries, etc. The data in chapters are also subdivided into sections and subsections, and each chapter, section and subsection is provided with a title. Titles in the table of contents also have page numbers to enable readers to locate the corresponding chapters, sections and sub-sections quickly. Moreover, the important names, subjects and words in the index also have page numbers for the same purpose. The assumption is that readers of textbooks may not want to read the whole textbook. Readers may also want to refer again and again to certain chapters, sections, subsections, names, and words in the textbook. Hence, the data are organized and stored in such manner as to facilitate easy search for, and location of specific data (chapters, sections, words, etc) in the textbook.

Exercise 12.2

Get hold of a magazine or a newspaper, and study how the data in the magazine or newspaper are organized and stored. Pay attention to such things as tables of content, titles, continuation instructions, use of photographs and drawings, page-by- page arrangement of different types of news (e.g. local news, foreign news, sports, etc), typeface sizes or fonts, advertisements, etc. Explain your findings.

12.6 Data storage in paper forms, registers, etc.

You have already learned about how data are often defined, structured and created in forms and registers (Unit 7 and 8). Common examples are visitors' forms and registers in offices. But there are many other methods for organizing and storing data in paper documents. For example, there are differences in how personal and business letters should be written. You also learned in high school about effective ways of writing different types of essays. Also, employers sometimes expect applicants for jobs to structure their resumes in specific ways. For each of these types of documents, there are usually more effective and less effective ways of organizing the data.

It is crucial for you to know how to organize and store data in different types of documents because you are learning data organization and management. You will learn more about effective strategies for different types of documents and contexts later on in this course, and in the other courses of your programme.

12.7 Data storage and retrieval in computers

You learned the basics of how computers organize and store data in Unit 5 - Data representation in the computer. You should review that unit again now. We continue here by explaining the strategies and methods of computer data storage and retrieval here. The discussion will be concluded in the next unit.

In Unit 5 you learned that computers use binary numbers to represent textual, numerical, image and sound data. You also learned that most computers use a binary coding system known as the American Standard Code for Information Exchange (ASCII). For instance, the ASCII binary code for the capital letter 'A' is 1000001.

Now, in computers each of the seven binary digits is referred to as a bit (from binary digit, and the complete binary number that represent a symbol is referred to as a byte. Accordingly, a human language word such as 'goat' will be represented by four bytes inside a computer or on a computer media. Of course, for the word 'goat' the four bytes are XXXXXXX, XXXXXXX, XXXXXXX, and XXXXXXX.

As explained earlier, data are stored in computer media as files, with each file containing bytes of data. The computer stores a byte of data for each and every natural language symbol, including spaces. Hence, the more the number of natural language symbols to be stored, the more bytes a computer must store on computer media. The size of a computer file can be described in terms of the number of bytes of data it contains, for example 2000 bytes (= 2 kilobytes) or 36,678 bytes (= 36.678 kilobytes). For example, all the characters in this unit, including the spaces, tables and figures, was stored as almost 51,232 bytes by the software that was used to save it on the hard disk. A software usually inserts different kinds of codes into a computer file as it is being stored, and the bytes for such codes are counted in the total for the file. Hence, the total number of bytes stored by other software for the contents of this unit could be lower or higher. Other terms that are used to describe higher magnitudes of bytes are shown in Table 12.1.

Table 12.1

7 bits	= 1 byte`	
1000 bytes	= 1 kilobyte (kb)	
1000 kilobytes	= 1000 kb	= 1 megabyte (mb)
1000 megabytes	= 1000 mb	= 1 gigabyte (gb)
1000 gigabytes	= 1000 gb	= 1 terabytes (tb)

At times a byte may comprise eight instead of seven bits.

12.8 Data in computer files and folders

On computer media, a word-processed business letter can be stored as a file with a separate file name. Similarly, a structured data file, containing data records and fields on the names; addresses, birth dates, etc., of a company's employees can also be stored as a single file. Furthermore, photographic images, graphic drawings, as well as audio and video recordings can also be digitized and stored as files.

The files created and stored on computer media are often also grouped into different directories or folders. A directory or folder is itself a computer file that may contain other files and folders. The relationship between a file and a folder on a computer is much like as a leaf is to a branch of a tree, also as a branch is to the trunk of the tree. For example, a tree comprises a trunk which contains many branches. In turn, each branch contains many smaller branches, and each of the smaller branches may contain leaves or fruits. This is illustrated in Figure 12.1.

Figure 12.1: How folders and files are organized for storage on computer media.
Computer

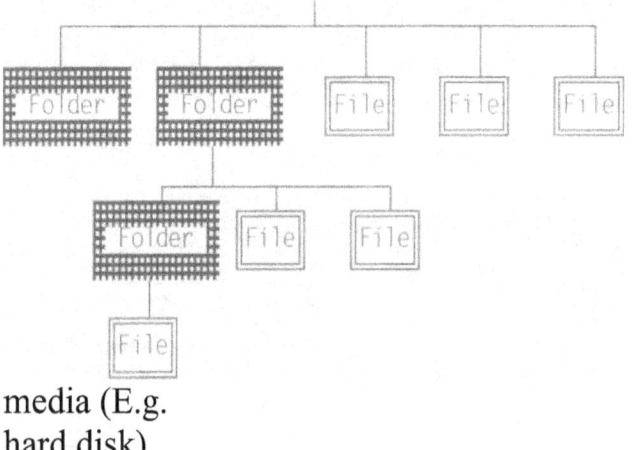

media (E.g. hard disk)

In Figure 12.1, the arrangement of files and folders is like an upside-down tree. Accordingly, the root of the tree is the media (hard disk) itself, at the top. On the root are folders and files. One of the folders at the first level also contains a folder and two files. Finally, the folder on the second level contains just one file.

Figure 12.2 also shows the usual display of the folders and files on a computer hard disk by the Windows Explorer software.

Figure 12.2: Hierarchical display of folders and files by Windows Explorer software.

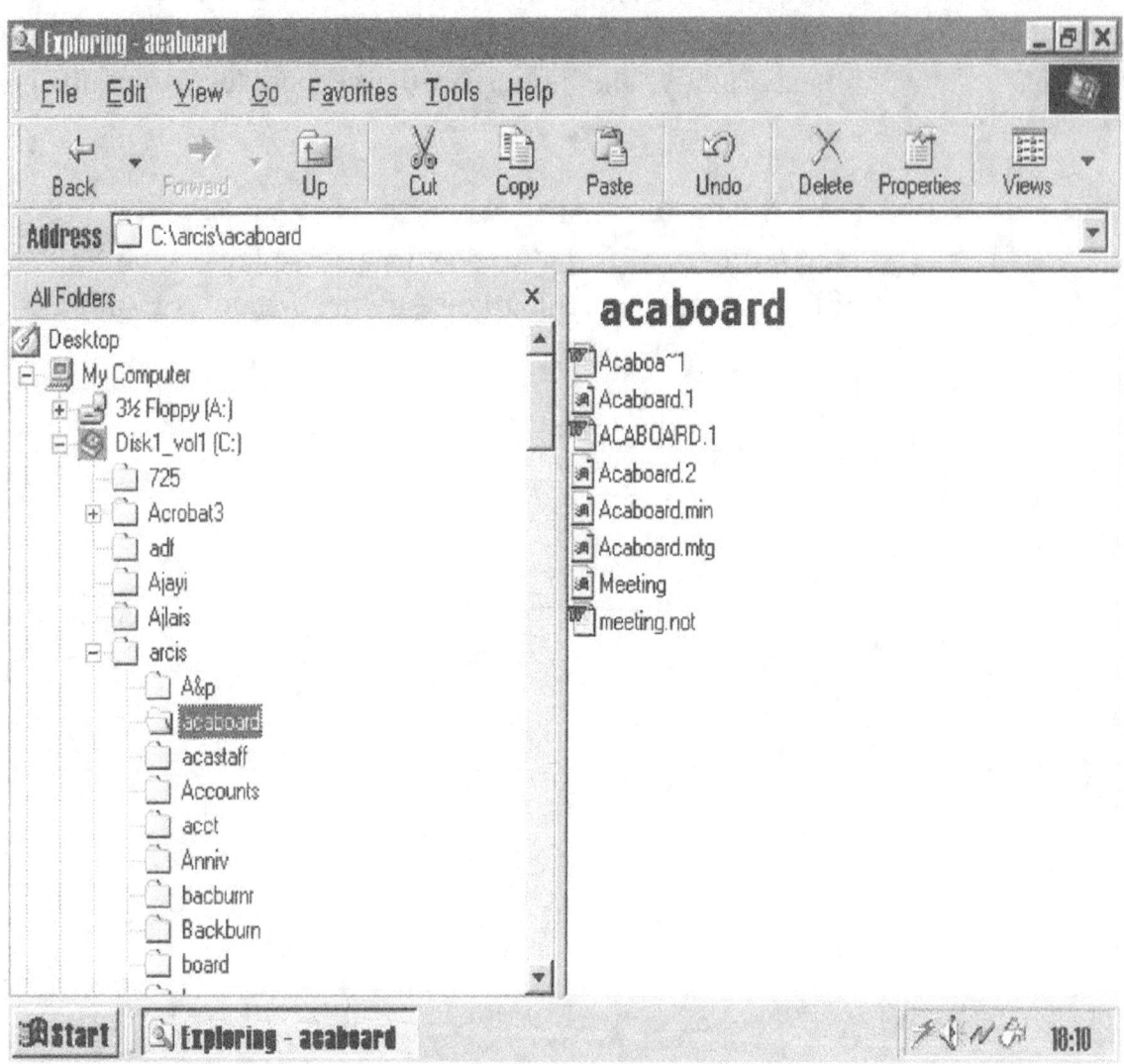

NOTES:

(a) Observe that the Object 'Desktop' is at the <u>Highest (First) level</u> of the hierarchy.

(b) At the <u>Second level</u> is the 'My Computer' object. This object is subordinate to 'Desktop' in the hierarchy.

(c) At the same <u>Third level</u> are both '3.5 floppy (A :)' and the 'Disk I vol.1' objects, both of which are subordinate to 'My Computer'.

(d) At the same <u>Fourth level</u> are the folders '725', 'Acrobat3', 'adf', 'Ajayi', 'Ajlais', 'arcis';

(e) At the same Fifth level, and under the folder 'arcis', are the folders 'A&p', 'acaboard', 'acastafr, 'Accounts', 'acct', 'Anniv', ' backburn','board', etc.

(f) Finally, at the Sixth level, and under the folder 'acaboard', are the files displayed in the right panel.

12.9   Data in computer databases

Finally, and as you will learn more about in the next unit, groups of data files or folders are sometimes created, grouped and linked together to form a database.

> **Exercise 12.3**
>
> Start a computer that uses the Window operating system. Run the Windows Explorer software to find out the folders and files that have already been created and stored on the computer's hard disk. Print a copy of what you see displayed on the screen. Select a file (not a folder) from the display by clicking on its name or icon with the mouse. What is the name and size of the file in bytes?

12.10 Conclusion

Data storage should always be carefully planned, just like all other data management activities. In fact data storage should be planned when data are being defined, structured, created and collected. Moreover, data storage should also be done with subsequent data retrieval in mind. Data can be stored on different types of media. Hence, the planning for data storage should also take into account the peculiarities, advantages and disadvantages of the different types of media.

12.11 Summary

In this unit, you have learned about the importance of data storage in the data management cycle, and the essential relationship between data storage and data retrieval. Data storage must always be done in such manner as to make data retrieval easy; else the data may not be accessible. Data can be stored in human brains as part of knowledge. Most data are however stored on paper media, but increasingly on computer and electronic media such as computer disks and tapes, and audio and video tapes and CDs.

Data can be organized and stored in different ways on paper media depending on the type and purpose of the document. Hence, there are different ways of organizing and storing data in story books, textbooks, newspapers, personal and business letters, forms, registers, etc.

Data are stored on computer media as bytes of data in separate named files. Such files are often also stored in directories or folders. Finally, groups of files and folders may be linked together to form a database.

12.12 Self-assessment exercises

1. Explain the relationship between data storage and data retrieval, using your own words examples.
2. Explain how data may be organized and stored in a (a) resume
(b) Newspaper
(c) Visitor note book

(c) CD-ROM (Compact Disk Read Only Memory)) disk.

DATA STORAGE IN COMPUTER DATABASES

Table of Contents	
13.1	Introduction
13.2	Objectives
13.3	Importance of data to organizations
13.4	Why a database?
13.5	What is a database?
13.6	Software for creating and managing databases
13.7	A few more database concepts
13.8	Conclusion
13.9	Summary
13.10	Self-assessment exercises

13.1 Introduction

In the previous unit you learned about data storage by computer. You learned that computers store bytes of data corresponding to the data symbols in human languages. You also learned that computers create files on computer media such as disks and tapes, and that computer files are often grouped into directories or folders.

On a computer, different types of software are used to create different types of files. A word processor software, such as Microsoft Word or Corel Word Perfect can be used to create and store a formatted text file on a computer disk. Similarly, spreadsheet software, such as Microsoft Excel can be used to create and store a file containing mostly numerical data. Similarly, software for analyzing statistical data, or for drawing graphs or paintings can be used to store other types of files.

However, the type of files of concern to us here are those created and stored by a type of software known as database management software or database management system (DBMS). As you will learn shortly, this type of software is used to create and manage data files containing structured data tables which in turn contain data records and data fields. Moreover, the software can be used to group the data tables, and link them with files created with other software, to form what is known as a database - hence, the name database management system (DBMS).

In this unit you will learn about databases, data tables and database management systems. You will also learn about why and how databases are created and used to store data. You learned about data tables, records and fields in Unit 7. Hence, by way of preparation, you should review that unit again now before going on.

13.2 Objectives

After studying this unit, you should be able to:

1. Explain the importance of database management to an organization or information system.
2. Explain the concepts of database, data tables, records and fields, as well as database forms, views and reports.

13.3 Importance of data to organizations

Organizations and information systems create and collect data and information as part of their day-today operations. For example, banks collect data daily on the payment and withdrawals of cash by their customers. Universities, colleges and schools collect data from their student's year in and out. Traders create and collect data when they record data about their purchases and sales. All organizations also acquire or create data when they receive or write letters to other organizations and people.

Let us now focus on just one organization, say the National Open University of Nigeria. To function properly, the university will need to collect, store and process data on many types of entities, including its employees, equipment, buildings, vehicles, activities, sales and purchases, projects, letters received, letters dispatched, office files, students, courses, examinations, graduation ceremonies, student associations, books in the libraries, study centres, tutors, tutorials, etc.

Now, notice that each type of entity is in the plural, meaning that for each type of entity there will be many instances or members of that entity. For example, there will be many employees, students, examinations, study centres, etc.

> **Exercise 13.1**
>
> List ten entities about which a wholesaler would want to collect, store and process data to obtain' information.

13.4 Why a database?

Data on each of the entities that were listed for the university in the previous section will invariably accumulate over time. As the years pass by, the volume of data collected and accumulated on each entity by the university will increase. Now, unless the university finds a way of organizing and storing the data, the data will grow into a mass of unorganized data from which it will be difficult or impossible to find specific data. If that happens the university will not be able to locate, say, data on specific students who graduated some years previously. What do you think will happen then? One possibility is that some people might claim that they graduated from the university, and the university will find it very difficult or impossible to confirm their claims.

This is the reason why the data created and collected by an organization, and which often accumulate over time, must be properly organized for storage and retrieval. Before computers became popular most organizations created, collected and stored data in paper documents - registers, forms, sheets, letters, printed reports, hand written memos, etc. Organizations also created office files, file cabinets and record centers for managing the data in paper documents. Eventually, paper files became too voluminous and demanded expensive storage space. So, organizations used microfilm and other types of microforms to store some of the data, particularly those not needed frequently. They did this by filming their documents and keeping the images on the microforms.

Nowadays, the computer provides great capabilities for storing and retrieving huge amounts of data very quickly on very compact computer media. The computer itself has also expanded the capacity of organizations and information systems to create and capture data. In other words, the computer has been contributing to the growth of data, as well as providing capability for effectively storing and retrieving the data. This is the main reason why databases are created with database management systems (DBMS) - to assist organizations and information systems in defining, capturing, storing and retrieving data in databases.

13.5 What is a database?

A database is as a set of computerized and linked files that have been created with a database management system for storing the data of an organization or information system.

As explained earlier, different types of computer software create different types of files on computer media. Although some of the files may be grouped into folders, the data in them are often not linked to the data in other files. Data in such 'stand-alone' files are usually difficult to link up for use together. By contrast, a database management system (DBMS) is designed to facilitate the creation and linking of files so that the files can be used together and at the same time. The files that are created and linked by the DBMS form a database.

Secondly, a DBMS is designed to create a particular kind of data file known as the data table. A data table is used for storing data on different entities in the form of records (rows) and fields (columns), as was explained in Unit 7. A separate data table is created for each entity. Hence, assuming that we want to create a database to store the data of the university mentioned above, an 'Employees' table will be created for storing data on employees, and a 'Students' table will be created for storing data on students. Similarly, other tables will be created for storing data on the equipment, buildings, vehicles, activities, etc., of the university.

Table 13.1 shows how a table created with a DBMS looks like. This is the same table that was first shown as Table 7.5 in Unit 7. The only difference is that there are now a few more records. So, you can now see why we recommended that you review Unit 7. Do so now if you have not already.

Your review of Unit 7 will have refreshed you with the following facts:

(a) Each row of data in a table contains data on each instance or member on entity. Each row of data is also known as a data record. Hence, there will be as many rows or records as are members of an entity. In other words, if there are 10,000 books in the library for which the 'Books' table (Table 13.1) was created, there will be 10,000 records of data in the table once the data on all books have been stored in the table.

(b) Each record of data is subdivided into separately meaningful portions known as data fields, and the names or labels of the fields are provided as the column headings. Each column or field contains data on the same attribute of each member of the entity. Hence, there will be 10 columns or fields if data were collected and stored on ten different attributes of each member of the entity. (There are only six fields in the books table of Table 13.1).

Table 13.1: A 'Books' table

Author	Title	Publishers	Year	Subject
P.K. Johnson	ABC of Gourmet Cooking	ABJ Publishers	1966	Home economics
.I.J. Anderson	Mirror in the sun	ABC Publishers	1970	Fiction
M.A. Tiamiyu	Data in Information Systems	Infoman Consult	1998	Data management
f. Akwaegbu	Understanding Pidgin English	Akwaegbu Ltd	2000	Languages
P.P Solarin	'O' Level English Simplified	Oni Books	2000	Languages
,,,	,,,	,,,	,,,	,,,

Exercise 13.2

List up to ten different attributes (e.g. names) of each of the following entities on which it will be important to collect data for the database of a secondary school:

(a) Teachers;

(b) Students;

(c) Parents/guardians;

(d) Office fides.

13.6 Software for creating and managing databases

Different database management software or systems have been developed for creating and storing data in databases. Among them are: Microsoft Access, dBase V for Windows, Visual FoxPro, Paradox, Oracle, DB2, etc. These DBMS can be used for creating databases to store different types of data - textual, numeric, image, etc. In addition, there are also a number of other database management software that are specially designed for creating and storing mostly textual data, such as the descriptions of documents and abstracts, as well as full-text documents. Examples of such software are Inmagic and Reference Manager. Another example is Micro CDSASIS for Windows which is distributed free to non-profit organizations by the United Nations Educational, Scientific and Cultural Organization (UNESCO). Micro CDSASIS is used by many libraries and information centres in developing countries.

13.7 A few more databases concept

You have already learned about the concepts of database, DBMS, and data tables, records, and fields. You now need to understand a few more.

(i) Form:

This refers to a pre-defined format for entering data into one or more data tables in a database. A DBMS can usually be used to design and display a form on the computer screen to enable data to be entered into the records of the table. For example, shown in Table 13.2 is a form that may be designed and used to enter data into records of the table in Table 13.1. Such a form can be used to enter data for each book, or to display the data for each book.

Table 13.2: A Database Form

\multicolumn{3}{c}{**Book Data Form**}		
Authors:		
Title:		
Publisher:		**Year:**
Subject		

(ii) **View:**

A view is a pre-defined way of viewing or displaying some or all the records and fields in a data table. A DBMS can be used to define and display different views of stored data on the computer monitor. For instance, Table 13.3 shows two different views of the data in Table

13.1. The first view shows only the data on the authors and titles of the books. That is, it shows the data in only two of the fields. The second view shows the title, year, and subject of only the books whose subject is 'Languages'. Many other views of the data can be pre-defined and displayed with a DBMS and stored in the database along with the tables. Pre-defined views are also stored in the database.

(iii) Query:
A query is a statement that instructs a DBMS to find and display from a database all data that meet some criteria. An example of such a statement is:

Display from the Books table the **author** and **title** of books published by 'ABC Publishers'.

You will note that a query comprises three main parts, as broken down below:

(a) Display from the Books table
(b) The **author** and **title** of books
(c) Published by 'ABC Publishers'.

The first line is the command to the DBMS telling it to display data from the books table. The second line indicates the fields to be displayed. Finally, the third line specifies the criteria or condition to be used by the DBMS to determine whether a record should be displayed. Queries are sometimes pre- defined and stored in the database.

Table 13.1: Two different views of the Books table

(a) **One View**

(Showing only data on the authors and titles of all books)

Author	Title
l'.K. Johnson	ABC of Gourmet Cooking
J.J. Anderson	Mirror in the sun

M.A. Tiamiyu	Data in Information Systems
T. Akwaegbu	Understanding Pidgin English
P.P Solarin	'O' Level English Simplified

(b) A second View
(Showing only data on the titles, year, and subject of only the books on 'Languages')

Title	Year	Subject
Understanding Pidgin English	2000	Languages
'O' Level English Simplified	2000	Languages

(iv) Query table:

A query table is created when a query instruction is performed by the DBMS. The query tables will contain only the records and fields from the specified data table that satisfy the criteria of a query. For example, the above query will result in the creation, by the DBMS, of a query table that contains on the author and title of just one record as shown in Table 13.4

Table 13.4: A Query table obtained from the Books table

Author	Title
J.J. Anderson	Mirror in the sun

Note that a query table is, in effect, a view of the specified data table, as explained earlier. Hence, a query table is sometimes also known as a query view. You will learn more about queries and query tables in Units 15 and 16 of these courses.

Exercise 13.3

Write out the Query table that will result when a DBMS performs the following, query: Display from the Books table the Title of books published before year 2000.

(v) Report:

A report is either a selective or a comprehensive list or summary of the data in records of one or more data tables in a database. The report sometimes includes calculated totals or averages for groups of records. A DBMS can be used to create one or more reports. Reports are normally intended to be printed, but can also displayed on the computer monitor. Figure 13.5 is an example of a report printed by the Microsoft Access database management system. Reports can also be pre-defined and stored in the database alongside tables, forms and queries.

(vi) Related database tables:

These are two or more tables the data from which are linked together such that records and fields in the tables can be viewed, processed or reported together as if the records and fields belonged to a single table. A DBMS can be used to create links between selected tables and query tables in a database.

(vii) Database system:

A database system comprises of a DBMS, a database created with the DBMS, other computer programs that are used with the database, and the people who operate or manage the database, such as data entry operators, data supervisors, database managers, etc.

> **Exercise 13.4**
>
> Design a data table to be used for storing the data on the attributes of the entity Teachers or the entity Students that you listed in Exercise 13.2. Write five fictitious data records in the table.

13.9 Conclusion

Database management systems are the most important software to data organization and management because they can be used by organizations and information systems to organize their data for storage and retrieval on computer media. Although other software can be used to create, process and store data, they often cannot be used to organize and link all the data of an organization or information system. Database management systems can be used to create databases containing data tables, forms, queries and reports, as well as to link the data tables with files created with other software.

Database management systems can be used to manage all types of data - textual, numeric, image and sound - that might have been created with other types of software. They can also be used to organize and store data collected in different contexts - in laboratories, field surveys, schools, businesses, etc. Accordingly, learning how to use at least one database management system is critical skill that you should possess as an information or data manager or computer scientist. We will teach you a few basic ideas about how to use DBMS in the next unit

13.10 Summary

In this unit, you have learned about the importance of database in the life of organizations and information systems. Organizations must organize the data that they create or collect, else they will soon be swamped by large quantities of unorganized data. Of course, it is always easier to find and retrieve specific data from organized than unorganized data. In fact, it is sometimes impossible to retrieve data from data that were not originally organized for storage.

In modern era, organizations usually use database management systems (DBMS) to create database for storing their data. DBMS is a software for creating databases. In a database, data are stored in data tables. A data table is a file in which data are structured into rows (records) and columns (fields). The DBMS is used to create the data tables in the database, and is also used to create and stored predefined forms, queries, views and reports in the database. Tables in the database can also be linked so that data in various tables can be displayed, printed or processed together as if they belong to a single file. Finally, the DBMS are also used to link data in the database with data created with other types of software, such as word processors, spreadsheets and graphics software,

13.10 Self-assessment exercise

1. What is a database? What is DBMS? What functions can a DBMS be used to perform in an information system?
2. Describe a database table with an example of your choice.

3. Visit an office in your neighbourhood to find out what problems the office encounters in storing and retrieving data and information system from the files.

13.12 References

Howe, D.R. (1989). Data analysis for database design. 2nd ed. London : Edward Arnold.

CREATING AND USING DATABASES: COMMON TASKS

Table of Contents	
14.1	Introduction
14.2	Objectives
14.3	Common tasks in creating and using a database
14.4	Creating a data base
14.5	Creating data tables
14.6	Updating a data table
14.7	Sorting records in a table
14.8	Creating and using indexes to data tables
14.9	Displaying data records and fields
14.10	Conclusion
14.11	Summary
14.12	Self-assessment exercises

14.1 Introduction

You began learning about databases and database management systems (DBMS) in the previous unit. In particular, you learned a few concepts in database management, including database tables, forms, queries, views and reports. It was stressed at the end of the unit that the practical ability to use at least one database management system for creating and using databases is a critical skill required by information or data managers or computer scientists.

In this unit we will explain some of the basic tasks that are performed when using a database management system (DBMS) to create and use databases. We will explain the steps involved in creating a database, and in creating a data table. We will also explain how records in a table may be sorted and displayed. This will provide you an opportunity to learn a few more concepts in database management. For instance, you will learn about the concept of a primary key field, and why each table in a database should have a primary key field. Finally, this unit will prepare you further for the practical computer sessions that you will perform with a DBMS in the next unit.

14.2 Objectives

After studying this unit, you should be able to:
1. Describe the common tasks in creating and using databases.
2. Explain the database table concepts of field name, field type and field width, primary key field, etc.

14.3 Common tasks in creating and using databases

Database management systems can be used to perform a large number of data management tasks. You will learn about five of the most common tasks in this unit. The five tasks are:

(a) Creating a database.
(b) Creating data tables.
(c) Updating records in data tables.
(d) Sorting the records in the tables.
(e) Creating and using indexes to tables.
(f) Displaying records and fields from tables.

14.4 Creating a database

Creating a database is the first task that you must perform when you begin to use a DBMS to create and manage a database. The database is created initially as an empty or blank container into which tables, queries, forms, reports, etc. will be stored or saved.

Hence, the process of creating the database is very simple: you only need to tell the DBMS three things: the type of database to be created, the name you want to call the database (i.e., file name of the database), and where (ie., in which folder) the database should be stored on a computer media.

14.5 Creating data tables

This entails two tasks:

(a) Designing the record structure of a table, usually on paper; and
(b) Using a DBMS to create and save the designed record structure in the database.
(a) Designing the record structure of a table

The record structure of a table is determined by the nature of the data fields that comprise each record in the table.

Designing the record structure of a table requires careful planning. Firstly, recall from the previous unit that you need to create a table in the database for each different entity - students, employees, purchases, etc., - for which data are to be stored.

Secondly, recall that for each entity you need to determine the different attributes for which data will be stored, so that appropriate fields can be created in the corresponding table.

Now, and thirdly, for each field that you decide to include in the table for an entity, you need to determine its:

(i) Field name;
(ii) Field type; and
(iii) Field width.

Field name (or Field label) refers to the name, label or heading for a field. A field name should be one that reveals the type of data stored in the field (e.g., 'Birth date' if the field is to contain the birth dates of people).

Field type (or Data type) refers to the type of data that can validly be entered into the field. Field types include:

<u>Character</u> (or Text): for a field that will contain different types of characters - alphabetical, numeric, special.

<u>Number</u> (or Numeric): for a field that will contain only numbers.

Date: for a field that will contain dates, such as birth dates, dates of appointments, or dates of sales.

Yes/No (or Logical): for a field that will contain either 'Yes' or 'No' data, or 'True' or 'False' data. For example, if a field of a table is named 'Passed English', valid data for the field will be 'Yes' or 'No'.

Field width (or Field size): refers to the amount of character spaces that will be provided for entering data in the field. An alphabetical character or a numeric digit occupies one character space each. Hence, if you specify a field width of 10 for a field named 'Surname', the DBMS will allow you to enter only ten characters for each surname in the field. Of course, for such a small field width, you will run into space problems if you must enter long surnames, such as 'Abiola-Thompson', in the field. The 10 spaces will be enough for entering only 'Abiola-Tho'. On the other hand, you will be wasting storage space on computer media if you specify an unnecessarily large field width for field.

Table 14.1 provides an example of a designed record structure of a table for some data on the employees of a company.

Table 14.1: Example of a defined record structure of a table

Field name	Field type	Field width	Remarks
Names	Text	25	
Address	Text	50	
Birth date	Date	8	Can be 8 (dd/mm/yy), or 10 (dd/mm/yyyy)
Salary in Naira	Number	6	Field width of 7 means that only salaries of up to 999,999 (excluding the comma) can be stored in the field.
Married?	Yes/No	-	Field width not required for this data type.
Staff ID code	Text	6	

You have now learned enough to be able to design the record structure of a table. This is what Exercise 14.1 requires you to do.

Exercise 14.1

Plan a table for storing the following data about the following attributes of applicants for admission to a university:

Names, Sex, Date of birth, Total number' of credit passes, Credit in English? Credit in Mathematics? JAMB Score, Course of Study desired, and Admitted?

Hint: For each field specify a short but informative field name, and the most appropriate field type and field width.

By doing Exercise 14.1 you have defined the record structure of a table for storing data on the applicants. This is because you have defined the types and amount of data that each and every record in the table will contain.

(b) Using a DBMS to create and save the record structure in the database.

Before you are ready to actually use a DBMS to create and save the record structure in a database, you need to do two other important things: You should

(i) make sure that a primary key field is included in the record structure of the table, and
(ii) select a name for the table to be created and saved in the database with the DBMS.

Primary Key field: Your design of a record structure of the table for applicants in Exercise 14.1 is not yet complete until you have a field in the record structure that will contain data to be used by the DBMS to identify each record in the table. In other words, you need a field whose data can never be identical for any two records in the table. Such a field is known as the Primary key field of the table.

Refer back to Exercise 14.1 to check whether you already have a primary key field. Let me help you with this. You will agree with me that two or more applicants can have the same names. So 'Names' cannot serve as the primary key field. Similarly, there is also no way of preventing two or more applicants from having the same sex, or the same birth date, or the same number of credits, or a pass in English, or a pass in Mathematics, etc. Hence, no field in the record structure that you have so far designed can serve as the primary key field.

One usual solution to the problem is to add an additional field with the field name 'Serial number' or 'Applicant number' to the record structure. This field can then be used to store numbers or codes that are unique to each data record. This is also the reason why universities assign unique matriculation numbers to students, and why motor registration centres assign unique plate numbers to vehicles, etc. For example, a university cannot prevent two or more students from having identical first names, middle names and surnames at the same time. Hence, in order to ensure that student and their records can be identified uniquely, universities assign matriculation or identity numbers to their students.

You should now include an 'Applicant number' in the record structure that you designed in Exercise 14.1.

<u>Table name:</u> You will be required by a DBMS to provide a different name for each table that you create and save in the database. Just like the field names, the name for a table should be short, and should reveal the type of records that the table contains. For example, a table for data on employees may be named 'Employees' or 'Staff or Personnel'. A good name for the table that you designed in Exercise 14.1 is 'Applicants'.

After designing the record structure of a table on paper, you can then use a DBMS to create and save the structure in the database. You will do this in the next unit, so keep safely your table design from Exercise 14.1.

14.6 Updating a data table

Updating is the word used to describe the process of adding, modifying or deleting data in a table. In other words, updating a table may entail (i) creating and adding new records to a table; (ii) changing the data in existing records; and (iii) deleting existing records.

Data entry into a table can be performed only after the table's record structure had been defined and saved in the database. Data entry may be performed as the data becomes available, for example, as a new applicant submits an application letter or a completed application form. Often the data are entered in batches of say, ten or fifty records at a time. The data might also be scanned into the records of a table using various computer input devices, such as scanner, cameras, microphone, etc.

DBMS software usually provides a form on the computer screen that can be used to enter data into the records of a table. Data are keyed or scanned into the form much like the manner one would complete a paper form. The software often also provides automatic checking of the data as they are keyed in. For example, if a data entry clerk attempted to enter alphabetical data in a field that is expected to contain only numeric data, the computer would beep a warning and reject the data.

14.7 Sorting records in a table

This task involves the rearrangement of the records in a data table in accordance with a specified criterion. For example, the records in a table containing data on visitors to a building will normally be the order of the date and time visitors enter the building. This is the natural time order. However, a DBMS could be instructed to sort or re-arrange the records in the alphabetical order of the names of visitors, or in the alphabetical order of the names of the persons visited. Similarly, the records in a table containing data on applicants could be sorted in the ascending order of the surnames of the applicants, or in the order of their ages, etc.

You learned about views of a data table in the previous unit (in section 13.7). To refresh your memory, a view is a way of displaying some or all the records and fields in a data table. Accordingly, each different sorting of the records in a data table is a different view of the table.

14.8 Creating and using indexes to data tables

A DBMS invariably has a facility for creating indexes to records in a data table. An index to the data in a table is similar to an index at the end of a textbook. In the same way as a reader of a textbook uses the book index to find quickly specific names, subjects or words in the book, a DBMS also creates and uses indexes to quickly find specific records in a table. DBMS usually use data in the primary key field to create what is known as a primary key index. However, data in the other fields of a table can often also be used to create other indexes.

The DBMS usually arrange the records in a table automatically in the order of the data in the primary key field. For example, if 'Student Number' is the primary key field of a table, the records in the table will be automatically arranged in order of student numbers any time records are added to, modified in, or deleted, from the table.

14.9 Displaying data records and fields

After data are entered into the records of a table, the DBMS can be used to display the records.

Records can usually be displayed in two ways: the datasheet method and the form method. In the datasheet method, the DBMS uses the table format to display the records, that is, in the form of rows and columns of data. As many of the records and fields can fit into a display window are displayed at a time, and scroll bars and cursor keys can be used to display more records or fields as desired. In the form method, the one record is displayed at a time and in a form, as shown in Table 14.3

14.10 Conclusion

Creating and using databases is a key aspect of data organization and management. The reason is that all types of data often must be organized and stored temporarily and permanently. Such data can be stored in both computer and non-computer (e.g. paper) media. However, computer databases provide a platform for structuring data into tables, records and fields, and for creating different queries, view, forms, reports, e.t.c, for updating, displaying and printing the data in the tables.

This unit has provided you further opportunity to learn about how data are organized in the tables of database. A few more concepts were explained, including field names, field types, field width, primary key field, indexes, and sorting. Finally, the explanation of some of the common tasks creating and using databases is intended to prepare you for the practical use of a DBMS on a computer in the next unit.

14.11 Summary

In this unit, you have learned about a few common tasks that you often must perform in order to create and use a database. You must first create a blank database, and then create and store tables in the database.

To create a table, you need to define its record structure. The record structure of a table is determined by the kinds of data fields that the records in the table will contain. Hence, in order to design a table, you need to specify its field name, field type and field width. You also must ensure that there is a primary key field among the fields that you define for a table. A primary key field is a field, the data in which can never at any time be the same for any two records in a table.

A table can be updated with data only after its record structure has been created and saved in a database. Data update may entail adding, modifying or deleting records from a table. Once data are stored in a table, a DBMS can be used to sort, index and display the records in different ways.

14.12 Self assessment exercises

1. Explain the importance of the record structure of data table.

2. Explain how you will use the index at the back of a textbook to find a word in the book.
3. Explain with an example of your own each of the following:
   (a) Field name
   (b) Data type
   (c) Field size
   (d) Primary key field

CREATING AND USING DATABASES: PRACTICE

Table of Contents	
15.1	Introduction
15.2	Objectives
15.3	Starting and using Microsoft Access
15.4	Creating a blank database
15.5	Relationship between MS Access and database objects
15.6	Understanding and using the Database window
15.7	Creating a database table
15.8	Updating the table
15.9	Conclusion
15.10	Summary
15.11	Self-assessment exercises

15.1 Introduction

In the previous unit we explained some of the basic tasks involved in creating and using databases. The aim was to prepare the ground for you to begin to gain some practical experience in using a database management system (DBMS) to create and use databases.

In this unit you will practice how to use a DBMS for performing a few basic tasks in database management. You will be learning to use Microsoft Access. You will use it to create a database and a data table. You will also learn how to update (ie, add and delete) records in the data table. Finally, you will learn how to use a readymade form (known as Autoform) to update records in the table, and how to sort records.

The explanations and practical exercises provided in this unit are not intended to turn you into an MS Access guru overnight. The aim is to whet your appetite by introducing you to some of the basic database management tasks that MS Access, or any other DBMS for that matter, can be used to perform. If you will be using MS Access for the first time, you will definitely need to supplement the exercises with additional tutorials in MS Access either at your study center or a commercial computer training center.

Of course, in order for you to do the practical exercises in this unit, you must have access to a computer on which Microsoft Access is installed.

15.2 Objectives

After studying this unit, you should be able to:

1. Use Microsoft Access to create a database, as well as a database table.
2. Use Microsoft Access to add records to, and delete records from a database table.

15.3 Starting and using Microsoft Access

15.3.1 Requirements:

This unit assumes that you can use a computer that runs the Microsoft Windows operating system. You might have acquired this knowledge in your computer fundamentals course which all NOU undergraduate students are required to pass. However, if you are still not sure of yourself, you may need some initial or additional training in computer usage at your study center or at a commercial computer training center in order to proceed.

You will also need access to a computer to practice the procedures described in this unit. Hence, for the rest of this unit it is assumed that you are sitting in front of a computer on which Microsoft Access is installed.

15.3.2 Starting MS-Access

(1) From the Microsoft Windows Desktop, (1) click Start, (ii) select Programs, and (iii) double click on the Microsoft Access icon or title from the Programs menu.

The window in Figure 15.1 is displayed.

(2) MS Access is now active, and you can use it to perform different database management tasks.
(3) Maximize the Access window so that it covers the entire screen.

Two options in Figure 15.1 are important at this point:

(i) You can click (Blank database] to create a new database. The database will be initially empty, hence the label 'Blank database'.
(ii) You can click [Open Existing Database] to open a database created previously.

15.4 Creating a blank database

(1) Select [Blank database] from the window shown in Figure 15.1, and then click [Create].

The File New Database window in Figure 15.2 is displayed.

(2) The 'FILE NEW DATABASE' window enables you to specify (1) the computer disk or tape on which the database should be stored; (ü) the name of the database, and (iii) the type of database. Hence, you are required to answer each of the following questions:

<u>Save in:</u>
<u>File name:</u>
<u>Save as type:</u>

<u>Save in</u> requires you to select a folder from the corresponding drop-down menu. Select 'My Documents' or '3'/2" Floppy drive' as desired.

<u>File name</u> requires you to specify a name for the database. Type an 8- character name for the database (e.g., 'Students' for a database to be used for storing students' records).

<u>Save as Type</u> requires you to specify the type of database to create. The default is always 'MS Access database'. Don't change this.

(3) Finally, click [OK] to create your database. The database will be created with the specified name in the 'My

Documents' folder or on the '3'/2" Floppy diskette', as you had selected. Note however that MS Access adds the extension mdb to the file name when it saves it on disk. The database will be an MS Access type of database. The database will at this point be empty.

Exercise 15.1:

Use MS Access to create a database to hold the data of a fictitious job placement company. The database name should be 'JOB-FIND'.

After the database is created, MS Access will display the window in Figure 15.3. This is the Database window, and the name that you specified for the database is shown in the title bar of the window. This window will also be displayed any other time you open the database with MS Access.

> **Exercise 15.2:**
>
> (a) Shut down MS Access, and use the Windows Explorer program to find the new database that you have created on either the hard or floppy disk, as the case may be.
>
> (b) Re-start MS Access after completing (a) so that you can continue studying and practicing the remaining part of this unit.

15.5 Relationship between MS Access and database objects

The relationship between MS Access, the databases created with MS Access, and the various tables, queries, forms, reports, etc., stored in each database is illustrated in Figure 15.4. Note that database, tables, forms, queries, reports, etc. are known as database objects.

The largest box represents MS Access. Various tools are available on its Menu and Tool bars for creating and managing data in various databases. In other words, MS Access can be used to create more than one database. In turn, each database holds various database objects, such as tables, queries, forms, reports, etc., that had been created and stored in the database.

Note also that although MS Access can be used to create different databases, only one database can be in use at one time.

Figure 15.4: Relationship between MS ACCESS and database objects.

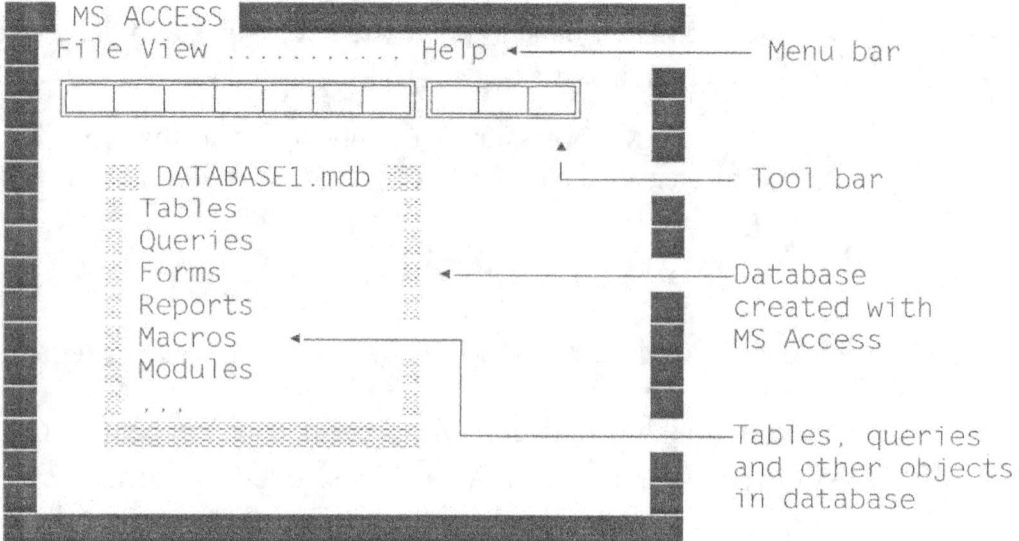

15.6 Understanding and using the Database window

In the Database window:

(a) You will find buttons for [Tables], [Queries], [Forms], [Reports], [Macros], [Modules], etc. These buttons provide access to sections of the database where the database tables, queries, forms, etc. that you create will be stored or saved. In other words, tables are stored together in one place, queries together in a different place, and so on.

When you click any of the buttons [Tables], [Queries], etc., the names of the tables, queries, etc., that had been created previously will be displayed in the while panel in the centre of the window. Of course no files will be displayed if no tables, queries, etc., had been created and saved in the database.

Exercise 15.3:

Click in turn each of the buttons [Tables], [Queries], [Forms], [Report].

(b) You will also notice the buttons [Open], [Design] and [New].

[Open] enables you to open a previously created and saved table, query, form, etc., for use.

[Design] enables you to redesign a table, query, form, etc. [New] enables you to design a new table, query, form, etc.

> **Exercise 15.4:**
>
> (a) Click [Tables], and then click [New]. Close the New window that is displayed to return to the Database window.
>
> (b) Click [Query], and then click [New]. Close the New window that is displayed to return to the Database window.

15.7 Creating a database table

The first thing you need to do, once you have created your blank database thereafter enter data records into it. To do this, do the following:

(1) Click [Tables]

(Existing tables in the database if any are displayed);

(2) Click [New]. The <u>New table</u> window is displayed (Figure 15.4);
(3) On the <u>New Table</u> window, select either <u>Design view</u> or <u>Table wizard,</u> and then click [OK].

15.7.1 Using the Design view option to create a table

The Design View option allows you to design a table from scratch.

(1) On the New Table window, select either Design view and then click [OK].

On selecting the option, a TABLE 1: TABLE window containing a table design grid is displayed (Figure 15.5). You can then specify in turn the following for each of the fields you want included in your new table:

(a) Field name (required);
(b) Data type (required);
(c) Description (optional).

(2) The following data types can be selected from the Data Type list button for the indicated types of data:

Data type Used for

Text: Short texts comprising alphabetical, numeric and special characters.

Memo: Long textual information.

Number: Numbers that would be used in calculations.

Currency: Monetary values or numbers requiring rapid calculations;

Date/Time: Dates or time data;

Autonumber: Sequential numbers automatically assigned by MS Access to successive records created in the table.

Yes/No: Yes/No or True/False data.

OLE: Image data, such as photograph, thumb print, signature, graphs, etc.

(3) Once you specify a field name, a lower panel is displayed where you can define the following other properties of the field:

- (a) Field size (maximum number of characters allowed for the field)
- (b) Format (how data would be displayed in the field)
- (c) Input mask (Required pattern for the data to be entered in the field)
- (d) Caption (Alternate caption for the field than the field name)
- (e) Default value (Value for field if data not entered into the field)
- (f) Validation rule (Rule for accepting/rejecting data entered into the field)
- (g) Required (Whether the field must contain data)
- (h) Validation text (Message to be displayed if validation rule is violated)
- (i) Allow zero length (Whether the field may contain nothing)
- (j) Indexed (Whether the field should be used to create index to the records)

(4) Setting or Changing Display Format of a Field [As explained in (5b) above]:

- (a) Click the field to display its current properties in the lower half of the New Table window;
- (b) Click the Format row;
- (c) Click the drop-down list button and select a predefined format or enter a custom format.
- (d) Some pre-defined formats from which you may select are available for some data types.

15.7.2 Using the Table Wizard Option

The Table wizard option enables you to borrow the record structure of any one of pre-defined tables which you can then modify.

(1) On the New Table window, select Table wizard, and then click [OK]. The Table Wizard window is displayed (Figure 15.6).
(2) On the Table Wizard window,
(a) Select [Business] or [Personal] category of tables;
(b) Click the table you want to borrow;
(c) Choose fields from the borrowed table (in the middle panel) that you want to include in your new table (send to the right panel).

NOTE: The properties of the fields that you include in your new table would have been pre-defined, but you can modify them later as you wish, using the Design View option above.

15.7.3 Setting a Primary Key

Each table must have a primary key field. The primary key field of a table is the field in the record structure of a table data in which will be used to identify each record in the table.

After defining the structure of your new table, you will be required to designate one of your fields as a primary key field. It is important that you designate a field for which no two records can have the same data, or else allow MS Access to create one such field for you. MS Access does this by adding an Auto number field to the record structure of your table. MS Access will then automatically enter a unique identification number in the Auto number field for each record that you add to the table.

To set the primary key for a table:

(1) If none of the fields that you have defined so far will satisfy this requirement, then create an extra field with the field name 'Serial number' or' ID number' in the record structure of the table.

(2) Click the field selector for the field you want. If you want more than one field to serve as the primary key field select the fields you want by holding down the CTRL key as you click the field selector.

(3) Click the Set Primary Key button on the Tool Bar.

[A key symbol appears against the selected Primary key field or fields].

15.7.4 Saving the record structure of the table

Save the designed table structure with an appropriate table name, for example, 'Applicants', 'Projects', 'Customers', or 'Employees'.

Exercise 15.5:

Use MS Access to define and save the record structure of the applicants table that you designed in Exercise 14.1 of the previous unit.

15.8 Updating the table

(1) After you save the record structure of your table, you can enter data into the table in any of the following three ways:
    (i)   Datasheet view;
    (ii)   Auto form; or
    (iii)   Custom form that you might have designed.

(2) To enter data in the Datasheet view, open the table you want to update and select Datasheet from the View menu.

(3) To enter data in your table with an Auto form, open the table you want to update, and click the Auto form button on the Tool bar.

Exercise 15.6:

(a) Use the Datasheet view to add five fictitious records to the 'Applicants' table that you saved in Exercise 15':5.

(b) Use the Auto form to add another five fictitious records to the 'Applicants' table.

(c) Delete one record from the 'Applicants' table, so that you are left with nine records.

15.9 Conclusion

The purpose of this unit has been to introduce you to Microsoft Access, through a series of simple computer exercises. Database management theory and practice is a very broad area of study in data organization and management. Hence, the exposure that we have provided for you in this unit is just the tip of the iceberg. Although this is sufficient for the purposes of this course, you should strive to increase your knowledge of database management concepts and skills as much as possible.

The creation and update of data tables are fundamental tasks in database management. This is because tables must first be created and updated with data before other data management tasks can be performed. However, data tables are not the only types of objects that you can create and store in a database. Once tables are created, you can proceed to design and save other types of objects in the database. As explained earlier, the other types of objects include forms (for use in entering data into tables), queries (for use in searching for data and information in a database), reports (for use in printing formatted reports on the data in the database, modules (for use in processing and manipulating data in the database). You should strive to learn about how to design and use these other types of objects on your own. It will be a very rewarding adventure indeed.

15.10 Summary

In this unit, you have learned about how to use the Microsoft Access DBMS to create a database. You also learned how to design and save the record structure of a data table in the database. You learned and practiced how Microsoft Access can be used to create one or more databases, and how one or more data tables can be created and stored in each of the databases. You also practiced and learned how to update a data table, ie. How to add, delete and modify data records in a table. Finally, you practiced and learned how to update a table using either the Datasheet or Auto form approach.

You should repeat the exercises until you are confident about each of them.

15.10 Self-assessment exercises

1. Use Microsoft Access to:
   (a) Create a database named 'EXAMS'.
   (b) Create a table named 'CANDIDATES' in the database for storing data about examination candidates in the following fields: Exam number, Names, Sex, and Address.
   (c) Enter 10 fictitious records in the table using the Datasheet approach.
   (d) Create another table named 'RESULTS' in the database for storing data about examination marks in the following fields: Exam number, English, Maths, French, Economics, Biology, Physics, Chemistry, History, and Government.
   (e) Enter 5 fictitious records in the table using the Auto form approach.
   (f) Delete the second record in table 'CANDIDATES'.

Figure 15.3: The Database window showing the created 'Newdatab' database.

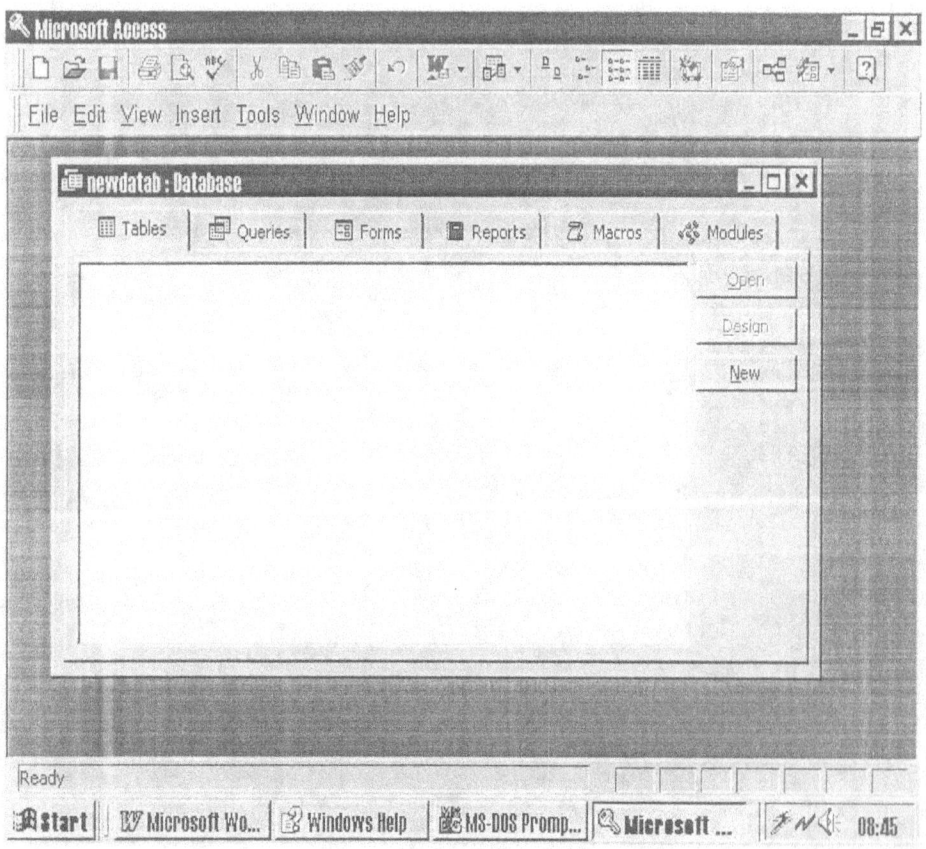

NOTES:

The Database Window shows buttons for different database objects: Tables, Queries, e.t.c.

The window also provides buttons for creating new objects [New], re-designing existing objects [Design], and for opening and using a selected object [Open].

When a new database is created it will initially be blank. That is, it will have no objects in it. Hence; the white panel in the middle of the window will display no objects when you click [Tables], [Queries], and e.t.c

Figure 15.4: The New Table window for selecting Design view, Table wizard and other method for creating a new database table.

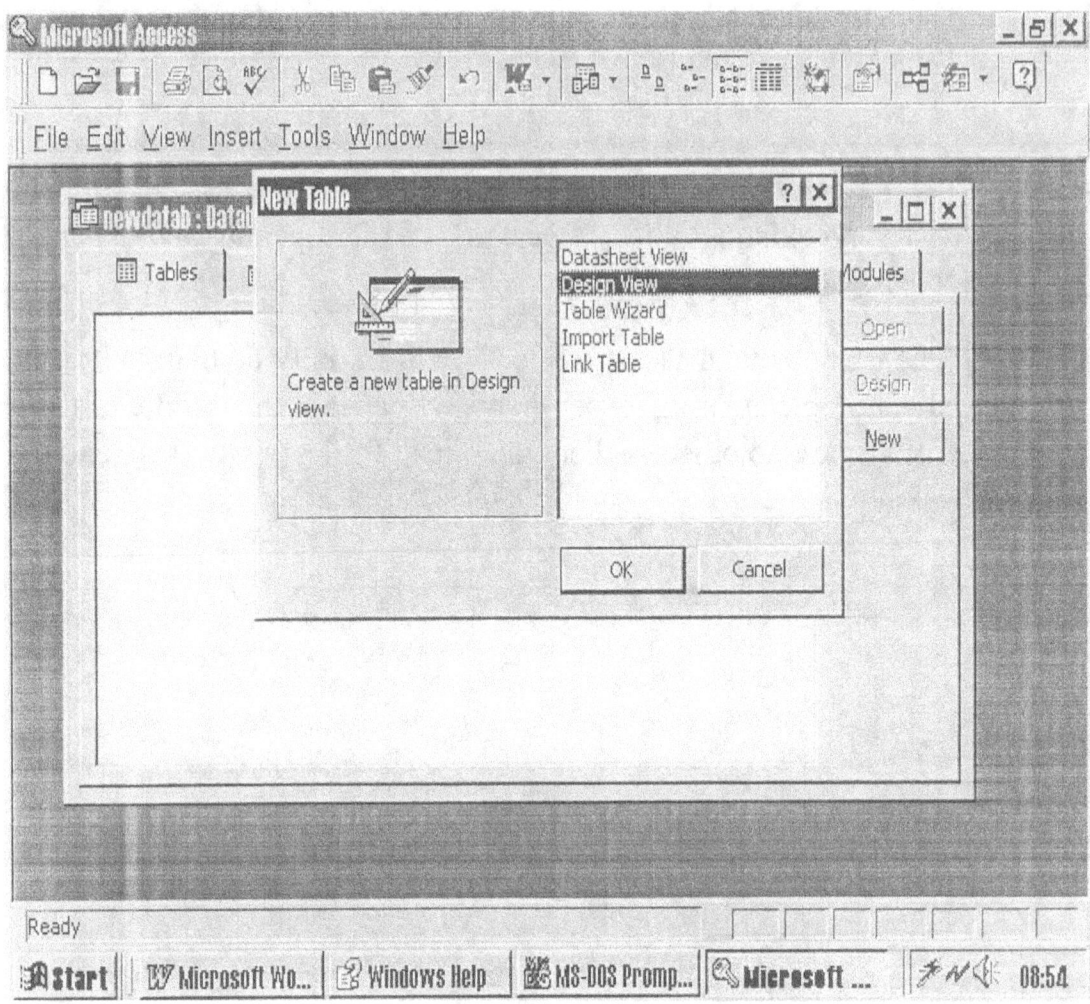

NOTES:

This window will initially have Datasheet view highlighted.

You will need to highlight the Design view, in order to design a table from scratch

You will need to highlight the Table wizard option in order to design a table from scratch.

After highlighting Design view or Table wizard, click [OK].

Figure 15.5: The Table1: Table window for designing the structure of a new table. (A few fields have already been specified)

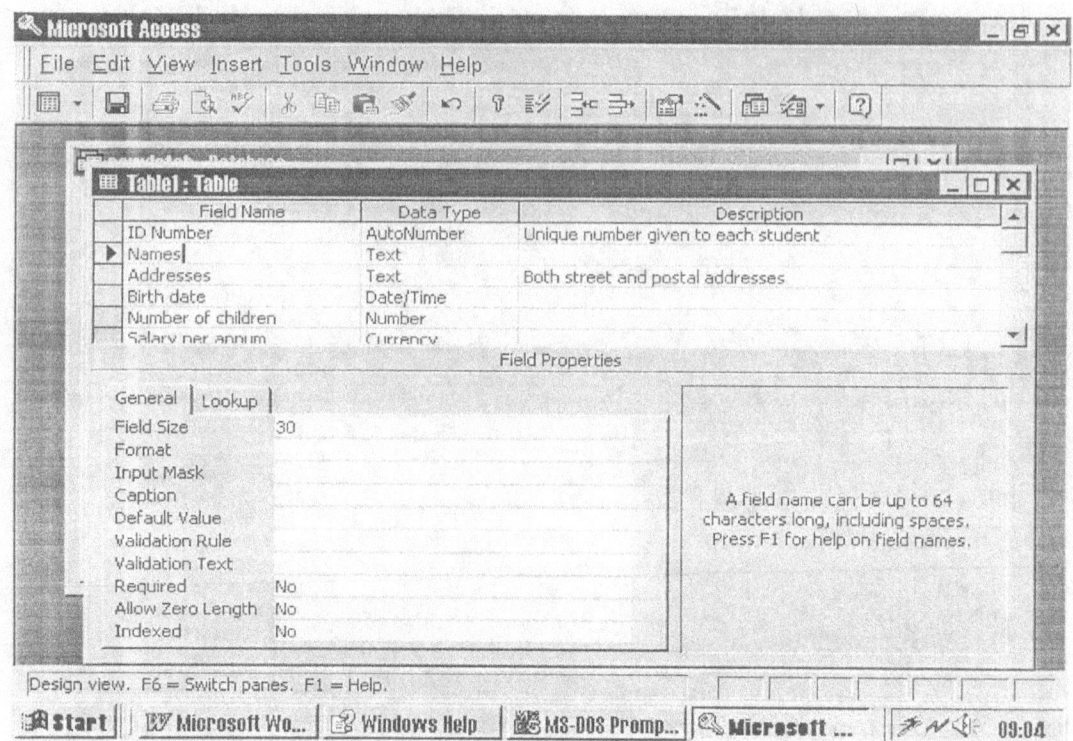

NOTES:

You are required to use this design window to specify the names and attributes of the fields that will be included in your new table. You can also use the window to change the attributes of the fields later.

You are required to enter data row by row.

(i) Enter the field name (e.g. ID Number)
(ii) Select the data type (e.g.Text, Number, e.g.).Use the list button to select data type.

(iii) You may omit the field description if you wish. The field description is used to describe the nature of the field.
(iv) Repeat steps (i) to (iii) for each of the fields that you want included in your table.

You can move to any row by clicking the row

You can insert a row before an existing row by clicking [insert] and then [Row] on the Menu bar.

You delete an existing row by clicking it and clicking [Edit], [Delete] from the Menu bar.

You can specify a field as a primary key by clicking the [primary key] button on the Tools bar, and then clicking the row of the field.

Figure 15.6: Selecting Table Wizard from the New Table window

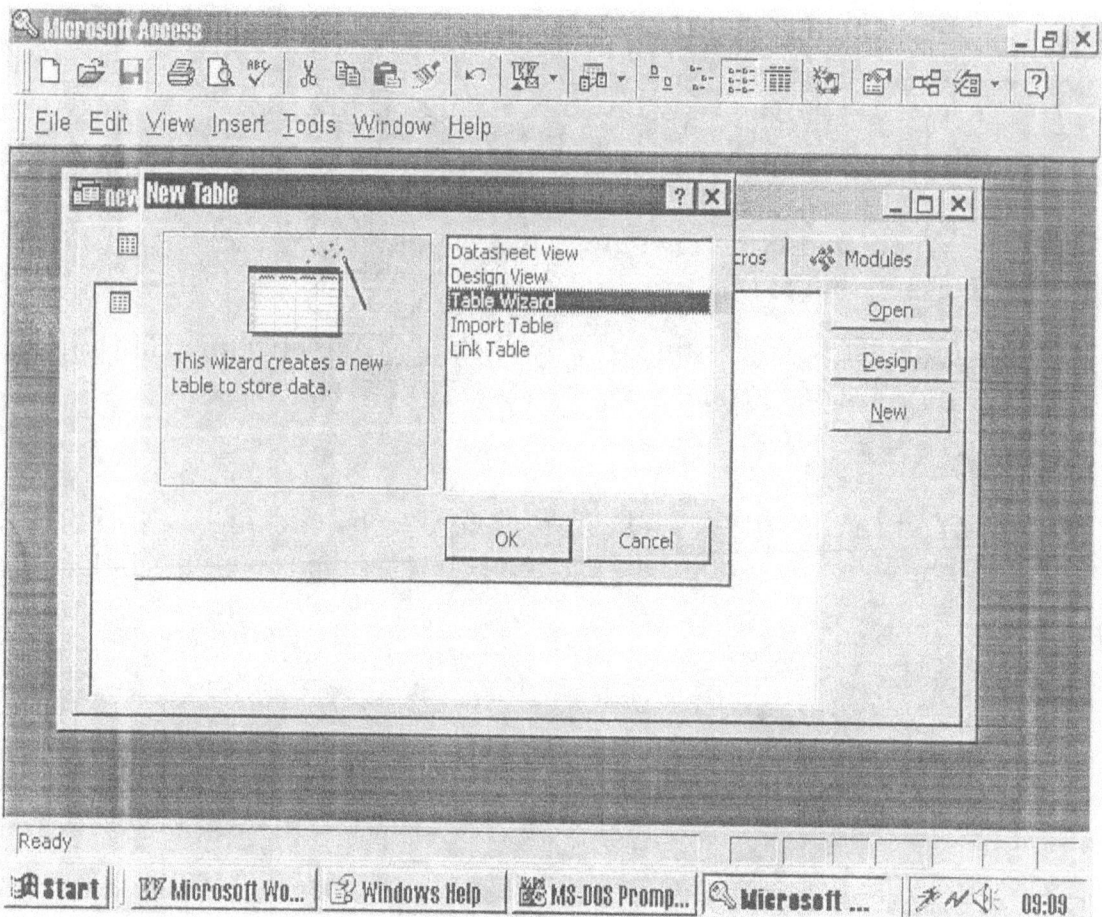

NOTES:

You should select the Table Wizard if you need assistance in designing the structure of your table.

The Table Wizard provides some readymade tables and fields that you can borrow to design your table.

Figure 15.7 (a): Table Wizard window for selecting tables and fields to borrow from the Table Wizard (Screen)

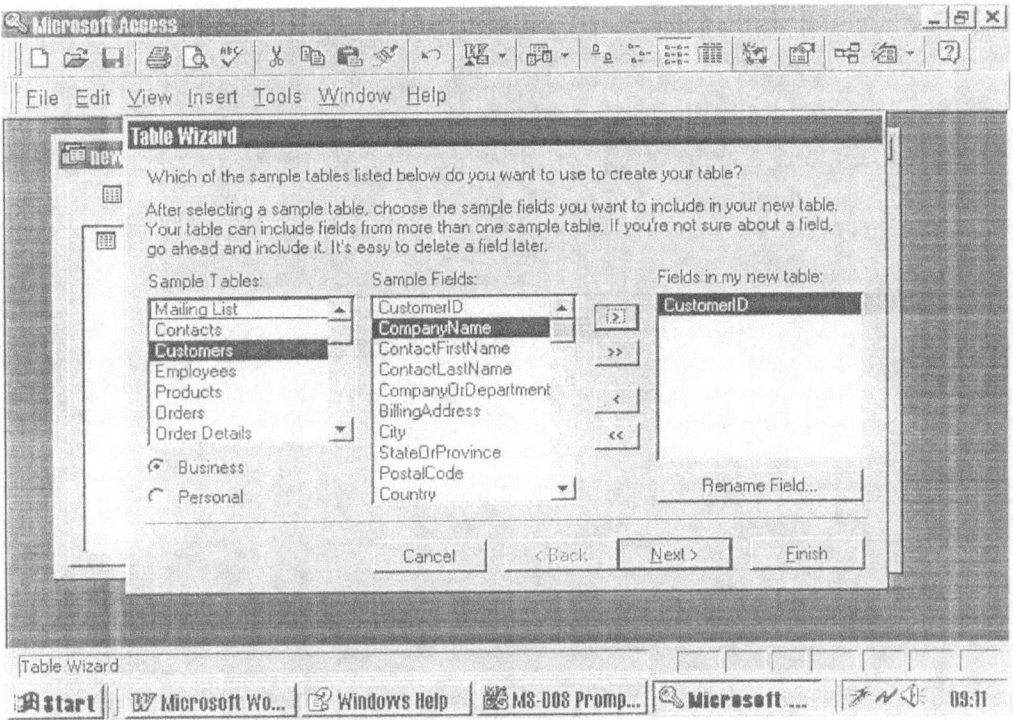

NOTES:

Business\personal options: The table wizard has readymade tables for creating tables for [Business] for [Personal] applications.

When you click [**Business**] or [**Personal**], the wizard displays the tables that you can borrow for business or personal uses in the leftmost panel.

In the above screen, (a) Customers table has been highlighted in the

leftmost panel,

(b) Customer ID has already been selected from the middle panel and sent to the rightmost, and (c)Company Name has been highlighted in the middle panel preparatory to being sent to the rightmost panels.

For each table that you highlight in the leftmost panel, the wizard displays in the middle panel the pre-defined fields for the table which you can choose from.

To borrow a table and fields:

(i)　　Select a table in the leftmost panel;
(ii)　　Select a field in the middle panel and send to the rightmost panel by clicking the [>] arrow

(iii) Repeat step (ii) for all the fields that you want to borrow from the selected table.

(iv) If you desire to change the name of any of the fields that you have selected,

  (a) click the field in the rightmost panel, (b) click the **[Rename Field]** button, and (c) Type a new name in the space provided.

Figure 15.7(b): Table Wizard screen for specifying the primary key (screen 2)

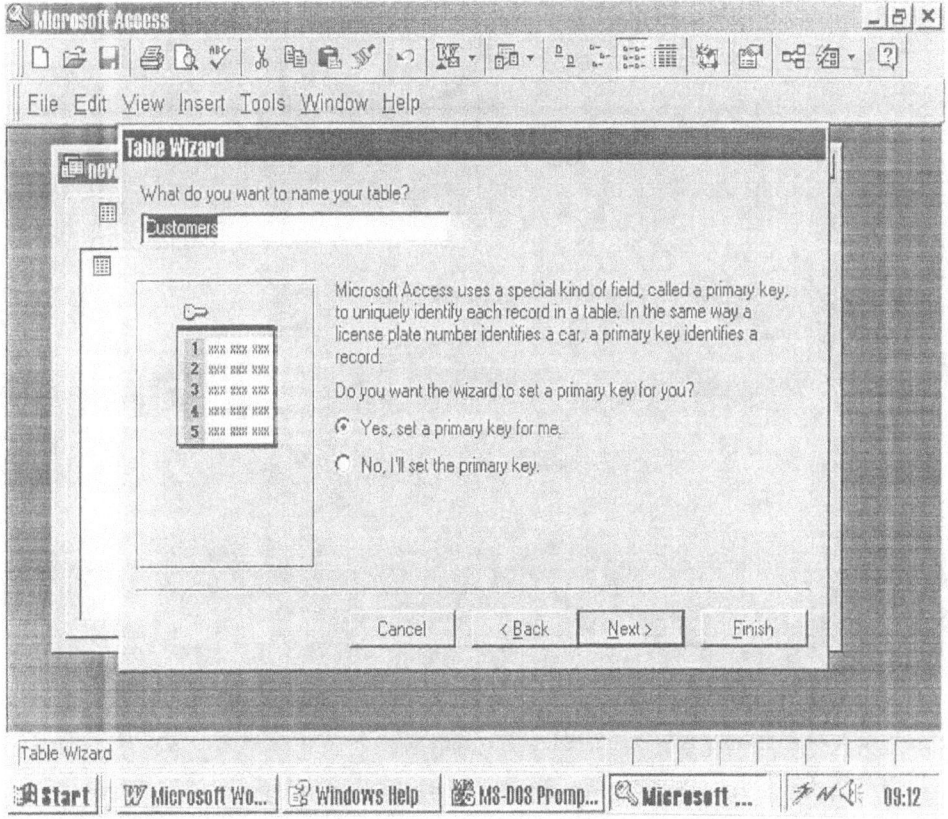

NOTES:

This screen is displayed when you click [Next] on the previous screen.

Each table you create must have one field that you designate as the primary key.

You may specify one of the fields that you had selected on the previous screen (screen 1). Or you may want the Table wizard to create a separate field to serve as the primary key

Let the wizard create a primary key for you, if you are not sure which field you want to use as the primary field. You can change the primary key later if you want

Figure 15.7(c): Table wizard screen for specifying relationship(s) between your new table and any existing tables in the database (Screen 3).

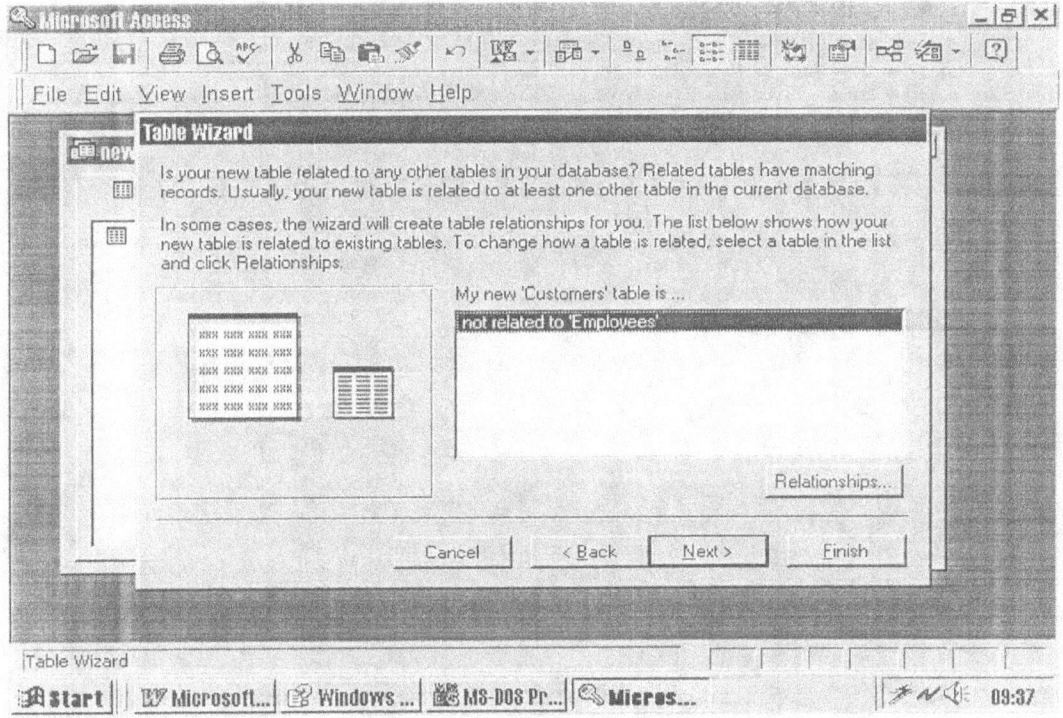

NOTES:

This screen is to enable you to specify any relationships that you might want to establish between your new table and any existing tables in the database.

Establishing relationships between tables may be too advanced for you if you are a beginner. So, you may skip this step, and just click [Next]

Figure 15.8: Table design window showing the Primary Key field.

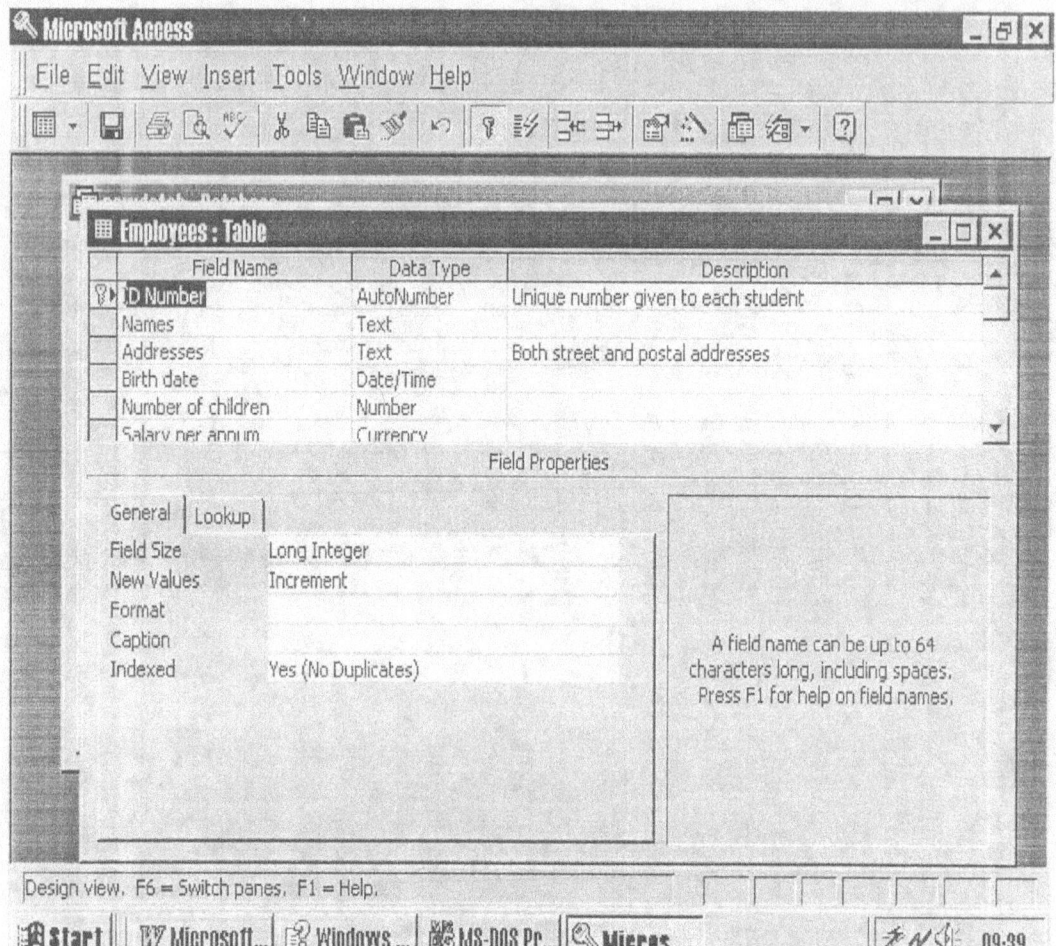

NOTES:

As noted above, each table you create must have one field that you designate as the primary key.

To specify a field as a primary key:

(i) Click the [primary key] button on the tool bar:
(ii) Click the field.

The symbol for the primary key (a golden key) is shown at the shown in the beginning of the row for the primary key field.

Figure 15.9 Data sheet view window for updating data in the employee's table.

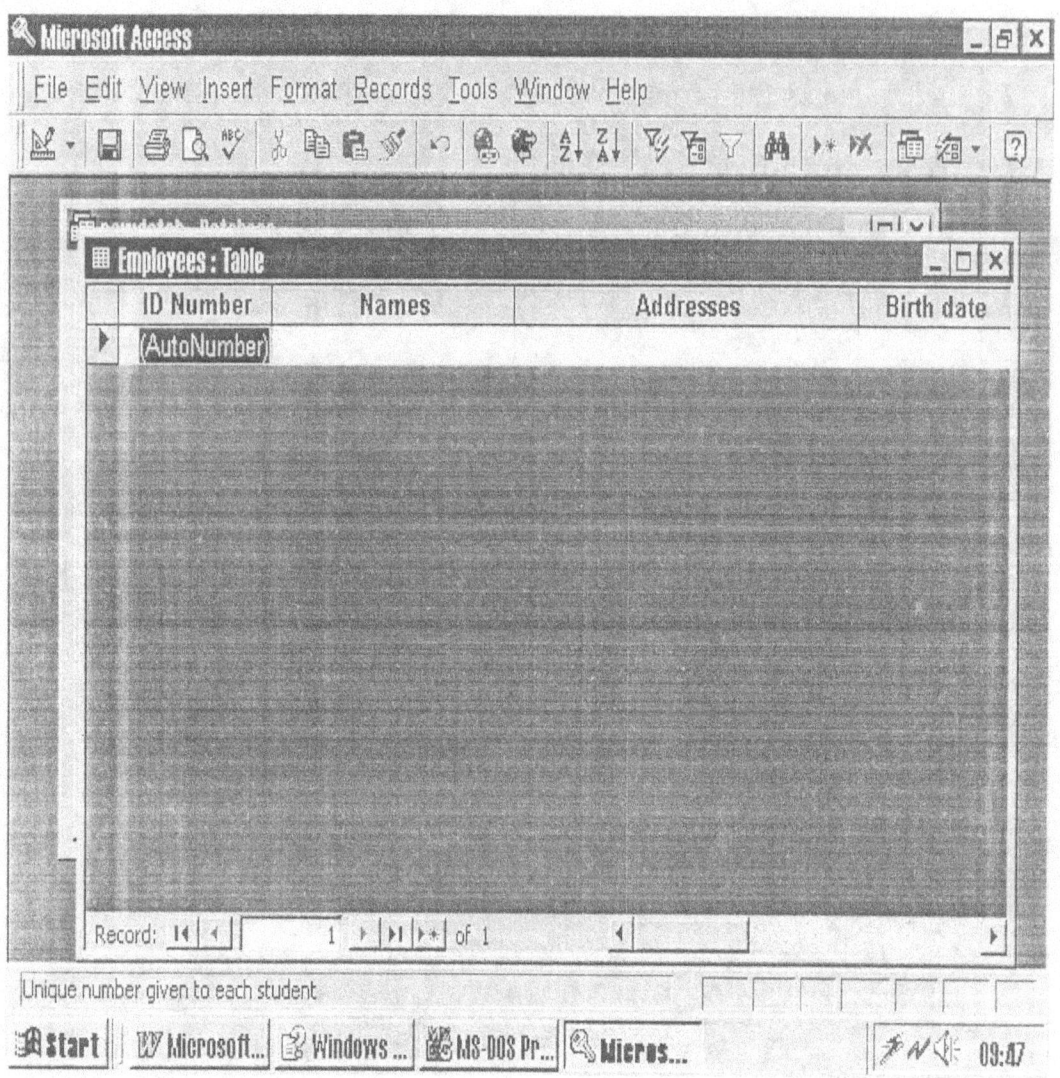

NOTES:

(1) The datasheet view enables you to update (add, delete and modify) data in a table.

(2) Each new or existing record in the table is shown in a row, and you update data by typing them in the appropriate fields.

(3) Only some of the fields and records in the tables will usually be displayed depending on the size of the Datasheet window.

(4) You can scroll between field by clicking or by using tab and Shift+Tab keys. You can also move between records by clicking records, or using the cursor control keys.

(5) You can delete existing records by highlighting the records and clicking [Delete] button on the tools bar.

(6) Note that data in the primary key field must be unique for each record. MS Access will permit you to proceed further if you violate this rule.

Figure 13.10: Using the Datasheet view to updating data in the first record.

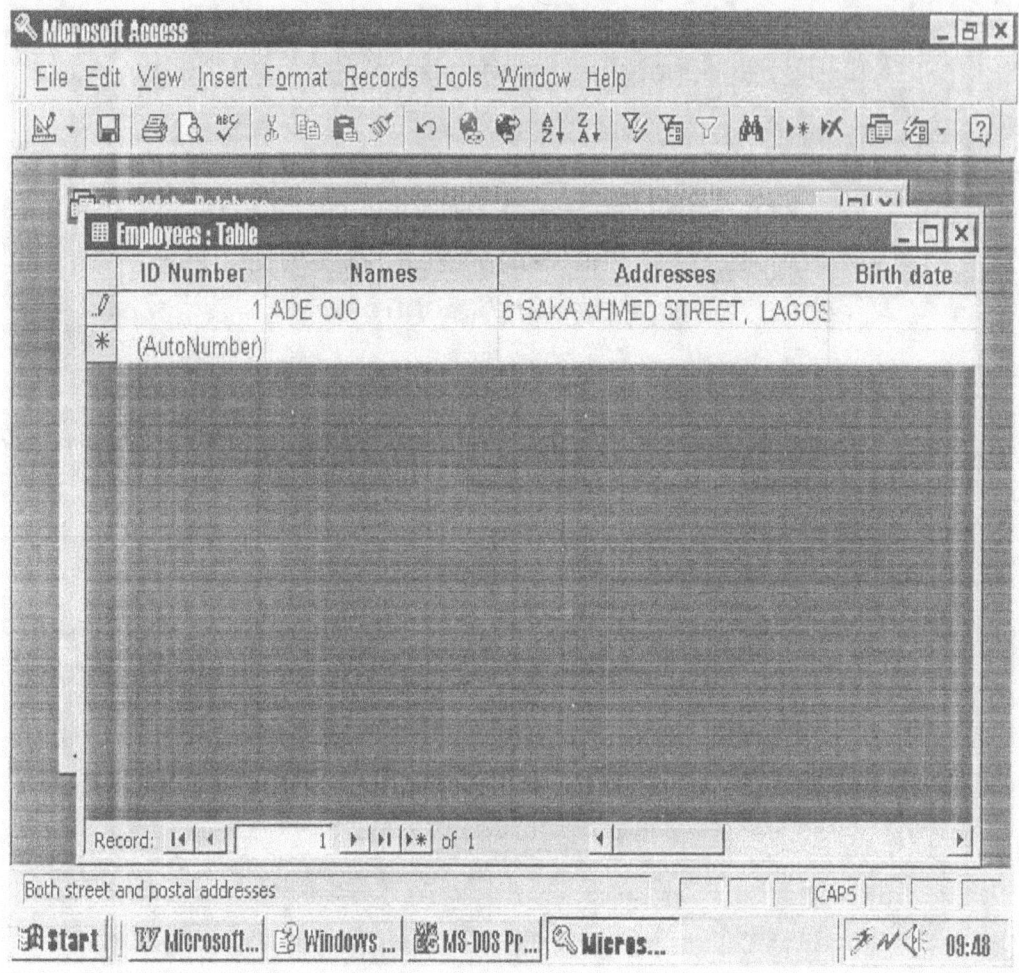

Figure 15.11 Using an Autoform to update data in the first record.

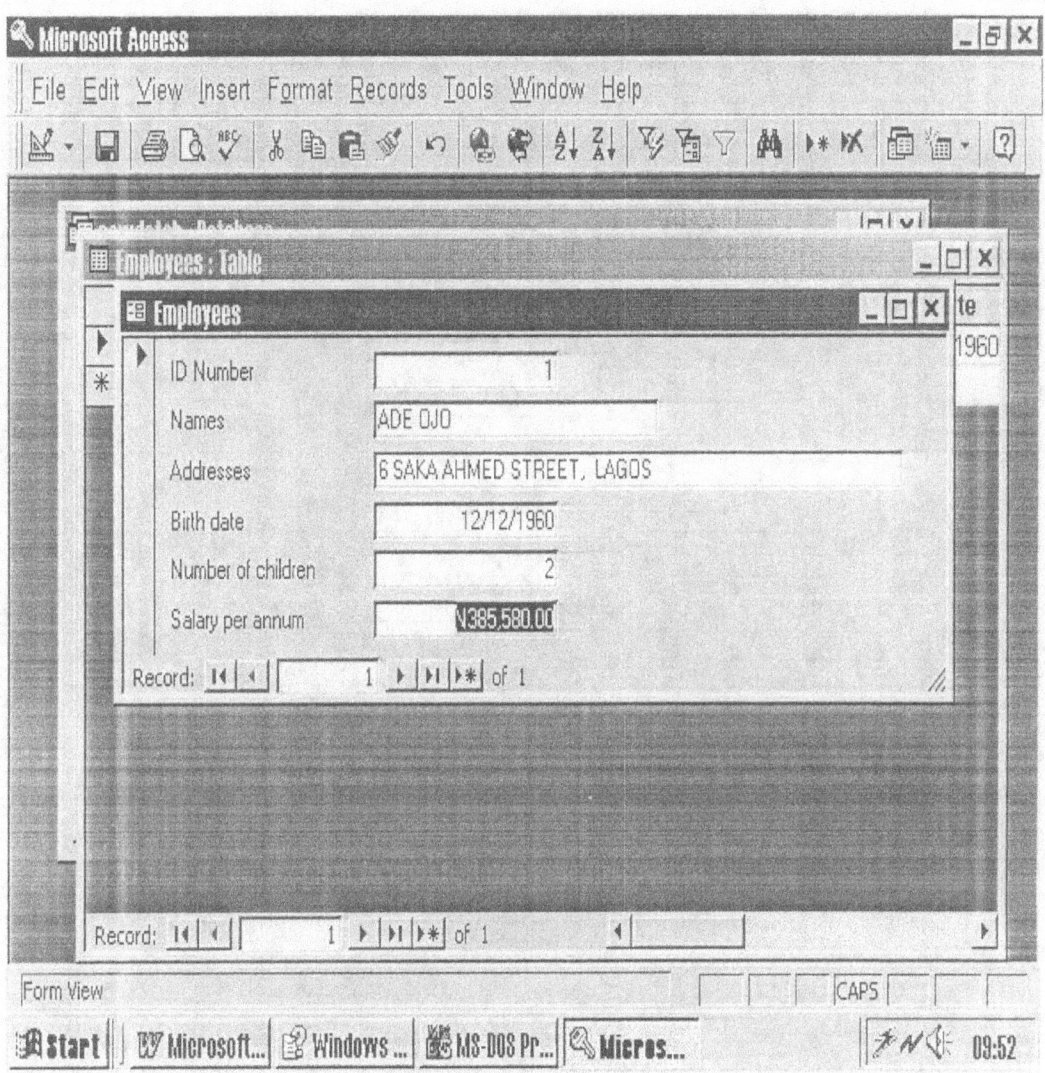

Figure 15.12: Using an Autoform to update data in new record.

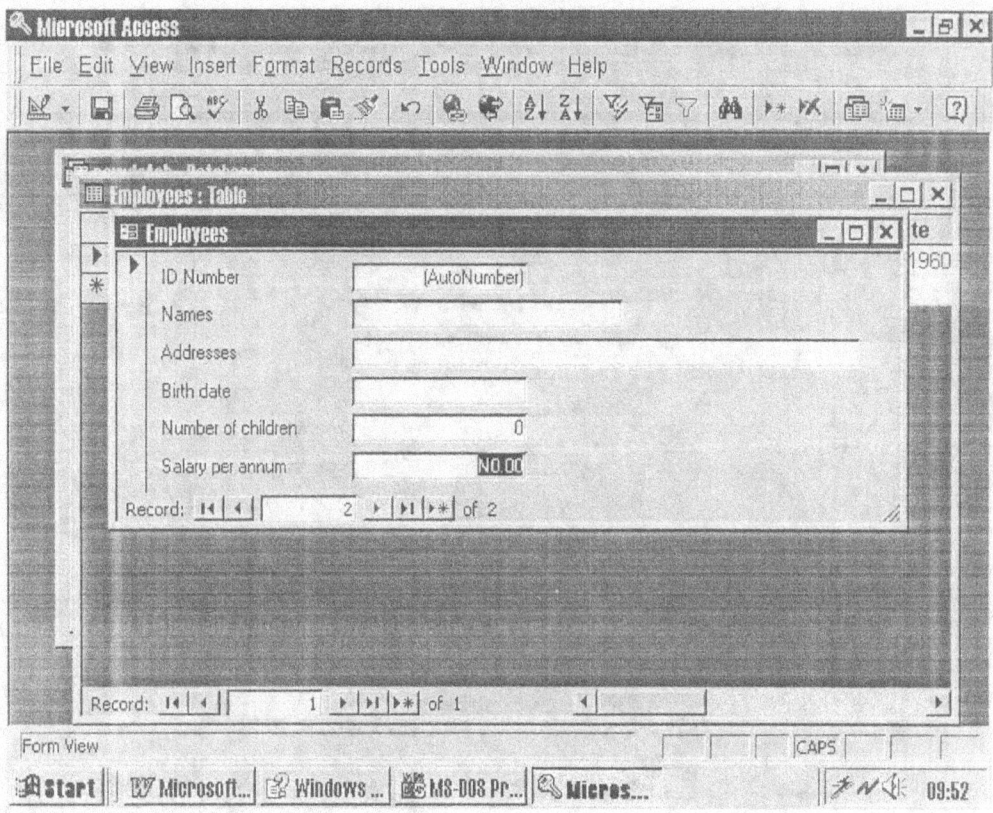

DATA AND INFORMATION RETRIEVAL CONCEPTS

Table of Contents

16.1	Introduction
16.2	Objectives
16.3	Context of information retrieval
16.4	Information retrieval from textbooks
16.5	Information retrieval concepts
16.6	Information retrieval from databases
16.7	Conclusion
16.8	Summary
16.9	Self-assessment exercises
16.11	References

16.1 Introduction

In the previous two units you learned about the processes that lead eventually to the storage of data in tables of databases. Before then, you had learned how data can be defined and structured (Unit 7), as well as arranged, grouped and modeled (Unit 8). Also, you learned in Unit 12 how data are or can be organized for storage in different types of media, particularly paper and computer media.

However, data organization and storage is never an end in itself. Data are invariably stored for subsequent use, otherwise there will be no point in expending resources to collect, organize and store the data. Indeed, all the ideas, strategies and tools that you have so far learned are geared toward facilitating the effective and efficient retrieval of data for use. In particular, the use of databases for storing data aims to exploit the processing speed of computers, as well as the internal logic of databases to facilitate data and information retrieval.

Accordingly, the effectiveness of data organization and storage can be assessed in terms of how effectively and efficiently the data can be retrieved from storage whenever needed. Data and information retrieval are important to data organization and management in that they provide the means for assessing how well the other management tasks, such as data definition, validation, collection and storage had been performed.

In this and the next unit, you will learn about basic concepts and strategies in data and information retrieval.

16.2 Objectives

After studying this unit, you should be able to:

1. Explain why the objectives of data and organization for storage are interwoven with those of data and information retrieval.
2. Describe the different data organization and storage strategies that can be used to promote data and information retrieval.
3. Explain the processes and strategies for searching for information from a book, and from a database table.

16.3 Context of information retrieval

Information retrieval is the process by which a person searches through a data store for some data or information. Note that the data store could be a textbook, a newspaper, a book index, a library catalogue, a telephone directory or a computer database. Note also that the person performing the search could be the one who created the data store, or someone else. In other words, data and information retrieval is the reverse of data and information storage.

Data and information retrieval enables information searchers to find, evaluate and use the data or information that data and information creators had created and stored in different types of storage media. Data and information creators include authors and editors (who write or edit books, reports, newspapers, etc), book indexers and cataloguers who create book indexes and catalogues, and database designers, operators and managers who create and update computer databases. Data and information creators often work within information systems. On the other hand, information searchers include readers of the books, newspapers and reports, and people who search databases for data and information.

Data and information retrieval provides a meeting point between data and information, and also between data and information creators and information searchers. On the one hand, people create data to express information. Such data are invariably recorded, organized and stored on paper, computer and other media using different kinds of strategies. For example, data are usually organized in textbooks into chapters, sections, sub-sections and paragraphs. Tables of contents and indexes are also provided. Data are often also organized into the tables of a database, with each table organized into records and fields. On the other hand, are information searchers who want specific data or information to use for various purposes, and are willing to search for information from various media and data stores. The important question is whether searchers will be able to obtain the data and information that they need by searching the appropriate data stores.

You will recall from Unit 3 that information systems provide facilities for acquiring, storing and processing and providing data and information for people, including information searchers. Data stores are examples of such facilities. Accordingly, one of the important functions of information systems is to implement appropriate strategies for creating, organizing and storing data so that information searchers can effectively retrieve data and information from the data stores as needed. However, toward achieving that goal, designers and managers of information systems must understand the processes of information retrieval. That is, they must understand how people search for data and information.

16.4 Information retrieval from textbooks

We will now introduce a few information retrievals concepts by describing the processes of information retrieval from a data store. Let us do this by describing the process involved in the retrieval of information from a textbook. Now, how do people search for and retrieve information from textbooks? What strategies and procedures do you yourself often use to find information from textbooks?

In order to search for, and retrieve information from a textbook you are most likely to go through the following process:

(1) Describe the information you want

You will, first of all, need to determine and describe the type of information that you want to find from the textbook. This may be a particular single word or phrase, paragraph, table, or any useful information on a topic or subject. You will then describe what you are looking with some data, such as <u>water yam</u>, or <u>Chapter two</u>, or <u>Figure 2.3</u> or <u>politics and corruption in Africa</u>. In information retrieval, what you want to find from a data store, and which you describe with data (such as <u>water yam</u>), is referred to as your search term.

(2) Determine where and how you will search

You can search for information in a textbook in different ways. One method is to leaf through the textbook page by page until; luckily, you stumble on a page containing the data or information that you want. However, you are more likely, to use any of the search aids or search tools provided in the textbook. The table of contents and the book index are two standard search tools in this respect. Search tools are invariably created to assist information searchers. You will note also that the table of contents is organized in the order of chapter numbers, and that the book index is organized in alphabetical order of important words or phrases in the textbook.

(3) Determine your search criteria

Let us assume that you have decided to search for your search term in the index. However, you still need to make up your mind as to how you will decide if a word or phrase in the index matches your search term. You might be looking for words or phrases in index that match your search term exactly, or you might be interested in words or phrases data that are approximately close to your search term in either appearance or meaning. In information retrieval, this is referred to as your search criteria. Your search criteria are the condition that must be met before you will accept that a word or phase in index is likely to lead you to useful data and information in the textbook. For instance, suppose you are looking for information on 'White Yam'. That is your search term. Your search criteria might then be any one of the following:

I am looking for a set of data (word or phrase) that is:

(a) Exactly 'White Yam';
(b) 'White Yam', or 'any other type of yam';
(c) 'White Yam or any root crop'.

Notice that the first of the above criteria is most specific, followed by second. The third criteria is the least specific. The more specific your search criteria, the lower will be your chances of finding words or phrase that can satisfy the criteria. Conversely, the less specific your search criteria, the higher will be your chances of finding words or phrases that satisfy the criteria. For instance, if (c) was your search criteria, you will accept and follow up on the following words when you come across them in the index: Yam, White yam, coco-yam, potato, cassava, and carrot.

(4) Perform the search in the data store

In this step, you will use both your search criteria to browse through the index. You will do this by inspecting words and phrases in the index, and then deciding for each word whether it satisfies your search criteria. Of course, being a human being, you might miss some words or phrase as you browse. You might also change your search term or search criteria as you browse. If you are lucky, you will find words or phrases that satisfy your search criteria. You will then note the page numbers corresponding to the words or phrases that you have found. Finally, you will refer to the various pages in the textbook, and locate where the words or phrase occur in the page

(5) Evaluate the data that you have found

Next, you will assess or evaluate the data and information that you have found on the various pages. You do this usually by noting and evaluating the other words, phrases and sentences associated with your search term in the textbook. For example, suppose your search term is 'white yam', and you have found it in a particular paragraph of the textbook. You will usually read the paragraph, as well as other nearby paragraphs toward gaining information about your search term.

(6) Evaluate the effectiveness of the search

Finally, after performing steps (I) through (5) above, you would probably reflect on the extent to which you had gained new data and information from the retrieval process. In other words, you will evaluate or assess the effectiveness of your search of the data store (i.e., the textbook). If your search was very successful in terms of providing you with valuable data and information, you would regard the data source as a 'good' source of information. You will also be pleased with the people or information system that created the data store. Conversely, if your search of the data store did not provide you with any or as much valuable data and information as you had expected, you would be disappointed with the data store. You might also be disappointed with the information system that created the data store. The important lesson for information systems and managers from this is that information searchers will often evaluate or assess a data source or an information system on the basis of the extent to which they (the searchers) are able to obtain valuable data and information from the data store created by the system.

Exercise 16.1

Suppose that I want to search for information in a book on tropical agriculture, and suppose that my search, term is 'white yam'.

(a) Which of the following search criteria is most likely to lead me on to, potentially useful or relevant paragraphs of information in the book, and why?
(i) 'White yam' and, nothing else;
(ii) 'White yam' or any other type of yam;
(iii) 'White yam', or any root crop (white yam! being a root crop).

(a) Which of the above search criteria is most likely to lead me onto potentially useless or irrelevant paragraphs of information in the book, and why?

16.5 Information retrieval concepts

You might have noticed that a number of important ideas or concepts in information retrieval were highlighted by the information retrieval process described in the previous section. The concepts include: search term, search criteria, where and how to search, information finding aids, effectiveness of search, etc. Let us explain some of these concepts more.

(i) Search terms and search languages

Search term is used to describe the data that one uses to describe the information one is looking for in a data store, for example 'white, yam' or 'economics'. The search term originates from a searcher's information need in that it is data that describe the need. A searcher may also have more than one search term, and may change search terms as he searches through the data store.

As explained in Unit 4, people create data by selecting and combining symbols from a natural or special language to represent or express information. The data are eventually stored in various data stores, which are subsequently searched by information searchers. Similarly, in order to retrieve information from a data store, a searcher is expected to use a language to create the search terms to be used for retrieving data and information from the store.

In particular, searchers must understand the language that was used when the data in a particular data store were being created. Searchers are unlikely to find required data from a data store even when the data actually exist if they use a language different from that used by data creators and information systems to store the data. Moreover, even when the searcher uses the same language, she has to be careful about what symbols (words, terms, phrases, key words, etc) are selected from the language to create search terms. For example, if a searcher's search term is 'aero plane', she may not be able to find 'aircraft' in a data store unless she is aware that she can use the latter word.

Accordingly, information systems and managers are expected to provide various tools that information searchers can use to understand the language that each information system had used for creating and storing data. For instance, tables of contents, book indexes or glossary of terms are standard tools usually provided in textbooks to assist searchers. Also, libraries, archives, records and information centers usually provide searchers with lists of the key words, subjects, author names, subject classification codes, etc. that had been, or would be, used for creating and storing data. Indeed, they often also create and provide different kinds of thesauri. A thesaurus is like a dictionary, in that it provides definitions, synonyms and related words for key words and subject terms that are used for creating and storing data in a library, archive or information center. Finally, data dictionaries are usually created to provide information about computerized databases.

A data dictionary usually contains information about the data fields of the data tables in a database. Finding aids and search tools are very useful because searchers can borrow words, phrases and subjects from them for use as search terms. Finally, information systems can also facilitate information retrieval by training new information searchers on how to search for information.

(ii) Known-item versus subject retrieval

Two major types of data and information retrieval can be performed in a data store. The first type of search occurs when the searcher knows precisely what he or she is looking for. For example, a searcher might want to know where in a book the name 'William Shakespeare' appears. Another example is when one wants to know if the novel Things Fall Apart by Chinua Achebe is in a library's catalogue. A third example is when someone is looking for the name of a particular person, Daniel Tobison, in a telephone directory. Such a search for information is referred to as a known-item search. The reason is that the searcher knows precisely what she is looking for. In such searches, the searcher is looking for some specific data, and will be satisfied when she is able to find the data that she was looking for in the library catalogue. The search will be considered effective if the required data were found. Conversely, the search will be considered ineffective or unsuccessful if the required data could not be found.

The second kind of search is known as a subject search or topical search. In a subject search, the searcher only knows the subject or topic of the information required from a data store, and is not sure whether there are any specific data in the store that can provide the information. For example, someone might be looking for books on economics in the library catalogue, but without having information about any specific book on economics. In this case, the search term will be a subject -'economics. Another example is when a tourist, who does not have prior information about any particular restaurant, uses a telephone directory to obtain information about the restaurants in a city. The subject or topic in this case is 'restaurants in the city'. A third example is when a person searches through the index of a book on Post-colonial Africa to find words or phrases that could point to relevant information on 'community development in West Africa'. In subject search, the searcher often does not have a particular set of data to look for in a data store, but will be interested in finding any data that will provide information on a topic or subject of interest.

Exercise 16.2

Pay a visit to an office, library, archive or record centre near you to find out the available data stores, and available tools for searching for data or information in the stores.

(iii) Effectiveness of information retrieval

We observed earlier those searchers often evaluate the effectiveness of their search of a data store by comparing the data and information that they are able to obtain with the data and information that they expected to find. Hence, searchers might praise a data store or information system if they succeed in obtaining valuable information from the data store. Conversely, they might blame the data store or information system if their search is unsuccessful.

However, it is important to know that the success or failure of any particular search for information in data store depends on more than what the information searcher thinks or believes. Factors that can affect the effectiveness of a search include the following:

(a) The quality of language that was used for creating and storing data in the data store;
(b) How the data in the store had been structured and organized by authors or information systems;
(c) The availability of search aids or tools for use by a searcher;
(d) The ability of a searcher to use the search aids or tools;
(e) The level of education and searching experience of a searcher;
(f) The care and time devoted by a searcher to the search process;
(g) The ability of a searcher to infer information from the data retrieved from the store;
(h) The searcher's initial expectation of finding valuable information from the data store compared to what was actually found.

You will notice that some of the above factors can be traced to the data store or information system, while others can be traced to an information searcher. Information systems and managers should not only be aware of these factors, but should also implement various strategies to ensure that information searchers are able to achieve reasonable success whenever they search for information in each datastore. For instance, information systems and managers can help information searchers by using appropriate languages for creating and storing data, by structuring and organizing the data appropriately, by providing various information search tools, by training searchers in how to search for information in the store, etc.

Exercise 16.3

Explain how each of the following can affect the effectiveness of information retrieval by an information searcher:

(i) The availability of finding aids or search tools for use by a searcher;

(ii) The searcher's initial expectation of finding valuable information from the data store, compared to what he/she actually found.

16.6 Information retrieval from databases

The information retrieval concepts that you have so far learned were illustrated with the process of information retrieval from a textbook. However, the concepts apply equally to information retrieval from other types of data stores. Let us now consider how data and information can be retrieved from a database.

You learned in Unit 14 that Table 16.1 below is how the data in a database table may be displayed as a data sheet by a database management system (DBMS).

Table 16.1: A 'Books' table

Author	Title	Publishers	Year	Subject
P.K. Johnson	ABC of Gourmet Cooking	AB.1 Publishers	1966	Home economics
I.J. Anderson	Mirror in the sun	ABC Publishers	1970	Fiction

M.A. Tiamiyu	Data in Information Systems	Infoman Consult	1998	Data management
T. Akwaegbu	Understanding Pidgin English	Akwaegbu Ltd	2000	Languages
P.P Solarin	'O' Level English Simplified	Oni Books	2000	Languages

Now let us consider how one might use a DBMS to search for data and information in a table. The procedure is usually more predictable than a person might search for information in a textbook. The reason for this is that database operations are invariably logically structured and organized. For instance, you learned in Unit 14 that the data to be stored a database are invariably delimited into records and fields. Hence, one can easily refer to a set of data in a table by specifying the record number and field name of the data.

Accordingly, you can search for data in a database table by performing the following steps:

(1) You select and open a particular database.
(2) You specify or select the table in the database that which you want to search;
(3) You specify or select the data field(s) in which you want to search for data;
(4) You specify your search criteria. This is the criteria to be used by the DBMS to search through the field(s) that you have specified.
(5) You specify how the DBMS should display any data that it finds on the screen.
(6) You instruct the DBMS to execute your instructions.
(7) You evaluate the data that the DBMS displays on the screen.
(8) You evaluate the effectiveness of the database and the DBMS in helping you to satisfy your information need.

Accordingly, in order to search for data in Table 16.1, one will first open the database containing the table, and might then request the DBMS to execute the following instruction:

Display Author, Title
from Table Books

Where Subject ='Languages'.

What this instruction says, simply, is that the DBMS should display from the Books table, the authors and titles of all book records for which the subject is 'Languages'.

You should satisfy yourself that the search term in the above instruction is 'Languages', and that the search criteria is "Subject ='Languages'". The information required by the searcher in this case is the names of authors and titles of books.

16.7 Conclusion

Information retrieval is what people perform when they search for information in various data stores such as books, newspapers, catalogues, maps, and computer databases. Such data stores are usually created by information systems. Designers and managers of information systems are interested in information retrieval because it provides them with the opportunity to assess the effectiveness of their systems and data stores. As explained earlier, information systems aim to provide facilities for providing data and information for people. Hence, an information system can be assessed in terms of the extent to which it enables information searchers to find the data and information that they need from the data stores created by the system.

16.8 Summary

In this unit, you have learned about the processes and concepts of information retrieval. Information retrieval is the process by which a person searches through a data store for data or information. Data stores include textbooks, newspapers, library catalogues and computer databases. Information retrieval provides a meeting point between data creators and information searchers. Information retrieval also provides a means for assessing the effectiveness of information systems in providing information searchers with useful data and information.

Among the important information concepts in information retrieval are: search terms, search criteria, search tools, and search effectiveness. A search term is the data that an information searcher looks for in a data store. A search criterion is the condition that data in a data store must meet before the data satisfies the data and information needs of a searcher. Search tools are devices often provided by information systems to help searchers to easily find information from a data store. Examples of search tools are indexes, tables of content, indexes and thesauri. Search effectiveness depend on a large number of factors that can be attributed to either an information searcher, a data store, or an information system.

16.9 Self-assessment exercises

1. Explain each of the following with an example:
   - (a) Search criteria
   - (b) Searching aid;
   - (c) Known item search;
   - (d) Subject search.
2. (a) What do you understand by the effectiveness of a search for information?

   (b) Explain how each of the following factors can affect the effectiveness of information retrieval from a data store:
   - (i) The quality of language that was used for creating and storing in the data store;
   - (ii) The ability of a searcher to understand and use a finding aid or search tool;
   - (iii) The care and time devoted by a searcher to the searching.

16.10 References

Sesoegel, D (1985). Organizing information. San Diego: Academic press.

DATA PROTECTION AND ARCHIVING

Table of Contents	
17.1	Introduction
17.2	Objectives
17.3	Importance of data protection
17.4	Storage media: hazards and protection strategies
17.5	Stored data: hazards and protection strategies
17.6	Conclusion
17.7	Summary
17.8	Self-assessment exercises
17.10	References

17.1 Introduction

People and organizations create, acquire and store data in different media in order to be able to retrieve and use the data for various important purposes, such as creating knowledge, making decisions or solving problems. Accordingly, people and organizations acquire and store paper documents, such as books, magazines, newspapers, reports, etc. Organizations also create databases for organizing and storing their data on computer systems and media. Libraries, archives and records centres also acquire and store books, journals, and other documents for subsequent retrieval and use by their patrons. Indeed, all the data management activities and processes that you have learned about in this course are geared either towards creating, organizing, processing and storing data, or toward retrieving and communicating the data for use.

A very important data management tasks in this regard is the protection of data and the media on which the data are stored. Data and media must be continuously protected to ensure that they continue to be available and accessible to the people, organizations or information systems who would need the data. Unprotected media and data can easily be lost to, or damaged by, natural or man-made hazards, such as flood, fire and environmental pollutants. Data can also be stolen or sabotaged by criminals, or can be lost through the honest mistake by the employees of an organization or information system. Any of these hazards can render waste all the time, money and effort that might have been expended by people, organizations and information systems to create, acquire, organize and store the data.

In this unit you will be learning about the different potential sources of hazards to media, documents and data. You will also learn about various strategies that organizations, information systems and information managers often use to protect their documents, data and media from disaster.

17.2 Objectives

After studying this unit, you should be able to:

1. Explain data protection, and its importance as a separate data management activity.
2. Describe the ways through which natural and man-made hazards can damage or destroy data and media.
3. Explain the strategies for protecting different types of data and media form hazards.

17.3 Importance of data protection

People, organizations and information systems expend significant resources towards performing various data management activities. You have so far learned about many of such activities, including creating, acquiring, validating, organizing and storing data. Their aim for doing this is to make the data available for future retrieval and use by themselves or others. You should also not forget one big advantage of data over other types of resources: the advantage is that data, unlike money, time, human effort, etc., can be reused many times over provided they are effectively stored and protected.

However, people and organizations especially in developing countries often fail to protect their data adequately, thereby exposing the data to various natural and man-made hazards. This is a reflection of their poor maintenance culture. Such people and organizations often fail to realize that adequate and continuous data protection is a must in order to ensure that the data continue to be available for retrieval and use as needed. Hence, although they might be willing to spend large amounts of resources in acquiring and storing data, they often are unable or unwilling to spend adequate resources to maintain and protect the data.

Stored data can be lost in either of two ways. Firstly, data will often be lost when the media on which they are stored are damaged or destroyed. Data storage media include paper, microform, video/audio cassettes, and computer disks, diskettes and tapes. Secondly, data can also be lost even when a media is still good, but the data on it have been erased, defaced or corrupted.

Information managers should be aware of all potential dangers to unprotected media and data. They should also know what to do to prevent the dangers from causing disasters to their expensive information systems and valuable data.

17.4 Storage media: hazards and protection strategies

The following are the various ways that media and data can be damaged or destroyed. Also provided are strategies that can be implemented to prevent such potential disaster to data.

Paper media:

(1) Paper documents eaten by rodents and insects.
(2) Paper documents destroyed by water from floods, leaky roofs, etc.
(3) Paper documents decayed by direct exposure to the environment.

Mice and rats, termites and other types of insects invariably prefer to live in the quiet confines of store houses where paper documents are kept. They often also feed and defecate on the documents, and inevitably pollute the environment of the store houses. Flood water from drains, leaky roofs or pipes and unclosed windows often cause rot, fading and discoloration of paper documents. Natural or polluted environments often contain impurities - dust, heat, acids, gases, water vapour, etc., that are usually harmful to paper documents. Such impurities can exist even in well-ventilated rooms.

Document store houses must be properly constructed and maintained to prevent these potential hazards from causing disaster to paper documents. Building standards exist for the construction of store houses for paper documents, and these should be followed. However, where ordinary rooms must be used as a store house, it is crucial to block all possible ways through which rodents and insects can have access to the rooms. The store houses should also be fumigated regularly. Regular checks should also be undertaken of the ceilings, doors, windows, walls and floors of store houses to identify and rectify potential sources of water leakage or seepage into the stores. Air conditioning of the store house is also highly recommended, although this may not be possible where electricity supply is unreliable. The alternative is to provide ventilation vents that are also protected against rodents and insects. Documents can also be shielded from direct exposure to the environment by putting them in wooden, steel or cardboard boxes, and by placing the boxes on shelves rather than on the bare floors.

Audio and video tapes

Video or audio cassettes made unusable or unreliable due to overuse, disuse or exposure to water, heat, dust, etc. Audio and video tapes are made from materials that are very vulnerable to humidity, heat, dust and magnetic fields. Humidity causes the tape to become damp and moldy. Dust on the tape can prevent access to the data recorded on the tape. Magnetic devices are used for recording data on such tapes; hence, the data can also be destroyed by strong magnetic fields created by other electro-magnetic devices.

Computer media

(4) Computer diskettes can be made unusable due to overuse, disuse or exposure to water, heat, dust, magnets, etc.
(5) Technical failure or crash of computer hard disk.
(6) Technical failure of poor-quality media.
(7) Natural ageing and degradation of media.

Poor quality disks, diskettes and tapes can fail to perform as required. Computer media can also fail at any time as a result of exposure to water, humidity, dust, heat and magnets. Such media often have a ferrous (iron) surface coating that can become rusty from exposure to water or humidity. Dust deposits can also make it impossible for stored data to be read from the media. Heat and magnetic fields can also damage the stored data. Moreover, the hard disk of a computer can fail at any time, making the data on it to become inaccessible and lost.

The usual strategy against these types of hazards is to maintain back up (ie., duplicate) copies of the data on alternative computer media at all times. Indeed, data that are updated daily should likewise be backed up unto other media at the end of each day. For this purpose, the hardware of a computer system can be designed (ie., set up) to have more than one hard disk so that data can be duplicated on the disks. The software of a computer system can also be configured to automatically back up the data on its hard disks unto other computer media or systems at scheduled times. Computer media such as hard disks, zip disks, CD-ROMs and tapes can be used for backing up data. You should note also that different computer media have different life spans. Hence, there should be scheduled copying or transfer of data from old to new media, and different schedule for each type of media.

All types of media

(8)   Stolen media.
(9)   Media destroyed by fire.
(10) Media destroyed through wars and vandals (e.g. rioting workers or students).

Media containing valuable data can be stolen. For instance, a stolen microcomputer system means that the hard disk is also lost. The thief might just be interested in the hardware, but data in the hardware will probably be more valuable and irreplaceable. Some thieves, such as industrial spies, might also be interested in having access to the information in the data. Fire is a very dangerous hazard in that it often destroys large quantities of media and data, as well as other facilities. Social riots can also lead to the looting and destruction of documents, computer systems and storage media.

The main strategy against these hazards is to create and maintain duplicate copies of documents, media or data, and to store the duplicates in a location far away from where the originals are stored. Duplicates can be stored in a nearby separate building, or better still, in a different branch of the organization. The process of duplicating the data and transferring the duplicates to alternative locations should be frequent for data that are updated frequently.

17.5 Stored data: hazards and protection strategies

As noted above, data could be damaged or destroyed although the media on which the data are stored is still intact. For example, data on paper documents could be erased, obliterated or forged. Moreover, data on computer media can often be erased or changed accidentally or fraudulently without any trace and without anybody being aware. You will recall that organizations and information systems usually create databases for organizing and storing their data. However, organizing data in a database is like putting eggs in a basket. Clearly, the basket (that is, the database), must be carefully protected from damage or destruction.

(11) Data erased or made inaccessible by computer saboteurs or criminals.

(12) Data on computers erased or made inaccessible by computer viruses.

Data on computer media can easily be erased by computer criminals hackers when they gain unauthorized access to a computer system. Computer criminals are person who gain access to computer systems to destroy software or data, or copy them illegally. Some computer viruses also erase data or make them inaccessible. A computer virus is a harmful software produced by computer criminals to cause damage to data or other computer software.

Organizations and information systems can protect their computer systems from computer criminals by implementing various strategies to prevent or restrict access to their computer systems. They can place their computers in a secured building or room, and restrict access to the building or room. Even employees may be required to obtain permission to enter the building or room, with penalty for any violations. Secondly, organizations and information systems can install sophisticated software in their computers to detect, prevent or raise alarm about any unauthorized attempts to access the computers. This strategy is particularly important in this age of networked computers and the Internet because computer saboteurs and hackers often try to attack a computer through other computers with which it is networked. Thirdly, organizations and information systems can install virus detection software on their computer systems so that viruses are prevented from infecting their systems. However, new viruses emerge frequently; hence, new versions of virus detection software should also be acquired and installed frequently as well.

(13) Use of non-standard computer media leading to inability to transfer the data into other media later.

Data can be lost when an organization or information system makes the mistake of using non-standard computer hardware, software or storage media to collect and store its data. 'Non-standard' here means that the hardware, software or media are not the same as those used by most other organizations or information systems. The danger is that, when the hardware, software and media become obsolete, or the company producing them folds up, it may become difficult or impossible to transfer the data from such media to other types of media, thereby causing loss of the data.

The lesson should be clear. Organizations and information systems should avoid using non-standard hardware, software or media for storing their data. More importantly, they should always use hardware, software and media that will allow them to transfer any valuable data to other hardware, software and media as needed.

(14) Bad data getting mixed with up good data in database due to negligence or absence of data quality control checks.

You will also recall from Units 10 and 11 that data validation and quality control help to ensure that only adequately accurate and reliable data are collected and stored by an organization or information system. However, the danger often is that people responsible for data quality control might not enforce the control always. This usual consequence is that inaccurate data get mixed up with accurate data, thereby reducing the reliability and value of all the data. Bad data among good data creates mistrust of the good data because one might not know which is good and which is bad.

The obvious strategy against this potential danger is to implement procedures and standards for ensuring that only adequately accurate data are collected and stored by an organization or information system at all times. This also means that the data control procedures and standards should always be followed, supervised or enforced.

(15) Data accessed by people who are not supposed to have them, thereby compromising their value.

The usefulness or value of some data or information depends on whether they are kept secret until used by authorized users. For example, the value to a firm of the documents containing its plans to surprise its competitors with a new product will decline if the documents fall into the hands of the firm's competitors. Such data and information are known as strategic data and information.

Measures should be taken to protect such strategic documents and data from unwarranted exposure or disclosure. For instance, most organizations store some of their documents in secret locations, and allow only their very senior employees and trusted secretaries to have access to such documents. Similarly, data stored in a computer system or network can also be protected by, firstly, assigning identification codes and passwords to users of the computer system or network. Secondly, users are classified in terms of the data that they can have access to. Hence, specific users are allowed to have access to only the data for which they are permitted.

Exercise 17.1

Examine the packaging of each of the following media. Read and copy the instruction as to the proper care of the media: (a) cassette tape, (b) computer diskette, (d) roll of film, (d) overhead transparency;

17.6 Conclusion

Data protection is a very important concept and activity. In fact, it should be considered as a key aspect of data storage. Data protection must be performed in order to ensure that valuable data stored on different types of media are secured from damage, destruction or inappropriate disclosure. The inability of a person, organization or information system to protect the data that it has spent a lot of resources to acquire, organize and store is a sign of poor maintenance culture. The basic lesson is that adequate attention should be paid to data protection as it is to data definition, creation, collection and storage. The message is that if you will need some data in the future, store the data, and if you must store the data, spare adequate resources to protect the data. It is always better to be careful than sorry.

17.7 Summary

Organizations and information systems acquire and store data in order to be able to retrieve and use the data later for various purposes. Such data, as well as the media on which the data are stored, must be continuously protected. Unprotected media and data can easily be lost to, or damaged by, natural or manmade hazards, such as flood, fire, environmental pollutants, criminals, etc. Data can be lost in either of two ways.

Data can be lost when the media on which they are stored are damaged, destroyed or stolen. Data can also be lost even when a media is still intact, but the data on it have been erased, defaced or corrupted. Storage media include paper, audio/video cassettes and computer media. Data and the different types of media are vulnerable to different hazards. Information managers should know about the different potential hazards to data and media, as well as about the appropriate strategies for safeguarding data and media from such hazards.

17.8 Self-assessment exercises

1. List the potential dangers to the data stored on computer systems.
2. List 20 different strategies that can be implemented to protect the data on different types of media.

17.9 References

Alegbeleye, B. (1994). Disaster Control Planning in Libraries, Archives and Information Centres in Africa.

Ricks, B.R.; Safford, A.J. and Gow, K.F. (1992). Information and image management, a record systems approach. 3rd ed. Cincinnati, OH: South-Western Publishing Co.

Robek, M.F., Brown, G.E. & Maedke, W.O. (1987). Information and records management, 3rd Edition. Encino, CA: Glencoe Publishing Co.

DATA ANALYSIS AND SUMMARIZATION

Table of Contents	
18.1	Introduction
18.2	Objectives
18.3	Data analysis and summarization
18.4	Data aggregation and disaggregation
18.5	Summarizing and analyzing textual data
18.6	Analyzing structured and numeric data
18.7	Computerized data analyses
18.8	Conclusion
18.9	Summary
18.10	Self-assessment exercises
18.12	References

18.1 Introduction

You will recall from Unit 1 that data are invariably created to express information, and that data are interpreted to obtain information to improve knowledge. The interpretation of data to obtain information for improving knowledge is referred to as data usage. However, data are often also used to produce other data. That is, data are often subjected to further processing before or when they are being used to obtain information. For instance, voluminous data might be summarized into less voluminous data by one person before being actually used by another. Numeric data might also need to be computed (ie, summed, averaged, etc.), or changed into other types of data (e.g., from numbers to graphs and charts) before they are actually used. These processes are referred to as data summarization and analysis. Data summarization and analysis can be done before data are stored, or after data are retrieved from storage.

Data summarization and analysis was identified in Unit 2 as a key data management activity in the data life cycle. Accordingly, you will be learning about various methods and strategies of data summarization and analysis in this Unit.

18.2 Objectives

After studying this unit, you should be able to:

1. Explain the importance of data summarization and analysis and a data management activity.
2. Describe the different methods for the summarizing textual data.

3. Describe the different methods for analyzing numeric data

18.3 Data analysis and summarization

Data analysis is the process of investigating and identifying the attributes or characteristics of a particular set of data. The attributes could be the information conveyed by the data, the types of symbols used for creating the data, the physical quantity of the data, the frequency of particular data or in the data, etc. For example, one might analyze the following sentence to determine its meaning, number of words, or number of characters, etc: 'The soccer match between the two clubs ended in a 0-2 upset defeat of the visitors'. One might also analyze the following numeric data to find their sum and average: '23, 34, 44, 12, 3, and 15'. Or, one might also divide data describing a distance (say, 135 kilometers) by another data describing time spent travelling the distance (say, 10 hours) to generate another data describing the speed of travel (ie., 13.5 km/hour).

Data analysis usually entails data summarization, transformation, aggregation and disaggregation. Data summarization is the process of reducing some voluminous data into less voluminous data. For example, a 100-page research report could be summarized into a 10-page version of the report. Data transformation or data conversion is the process of converting one type of data into another. An example is when temperature data is converted from Celsius to Fahrenheit units. Another example is when pure numbers are converted into logarithmic numbers. This type of data transformation or conversion usually involves numeric data, and requires the use of mathematical or statistical formula. However, numeric data can often also be transformed or converted into textual or graphical data. For instance, some sentences (textual data) could be written to express the information expressed by numeric data, and vice versa. Or, a chart (graphical data) could be drawn to represent the information expressed by some textual or numeric data.

18.4 Data aggregation and disaggregation

Data aggregation refers to the process of merging two or more originally separate sets of data into a single set of data. For example, election results in The United States are invariably collated or aggregated from polling stations to get the results for electoral wards, and then the results from wards are aggregated to get the results of local government areas, and so on.

Data disaggregation refers to the process of breaking or decomposing some data into two or more separate data sets. Note however that data disaggregation is usually much more difficult than data aggregation. For instance, once three numbers have been added up to get another number, it will be impossible to break or decompose the sum into the original numbers unless one also knows at least two of the original numbers.

Data aggregation during and after data collection

Data may be aggregated during or after collection. Compare for instance, the data that can be collected from housewives with the following alternative sets of questions:

(1)   How much do you spend on cooking oil per week?

Compared with

(2 a)   How much do you spend on palm oil per week?

(2 b)   How much do you spend on groundnut oil per week?

(2 c)   How much do you spend on all other types of cooking oil per week?

You will agree that, the first question will yield data that pertain to all kinds of cooking oils purchased by housewives - palm oil, groundnut oil, coconut oil, sunflower oil, etc. With such data, one will not later be able to know how much each housewife spends on any particular type of cooking oil. By contrast, the second set of three questions will at least allow one to know how much each housewife spends on each of the three types of cooking oil.

Data can also be aggregated after being collected. In the above example, one can calculate the total weekly expenditure on all types of cooking oil by summing the data provided to the second set of questions by the house wives.

18.5 Summarizing and analyzing textual data

As explained above, data summarization entails reducing some voluminous data into less voluminous data. Data summarization is often performed with textual data which often tend to be voluminous. For instance, the data in a whole book, or in a chapter of the book, or in a paragraph of a chapter, could be summarized into less voluminous textual data such as a single sentence, or a subject phrase. Information scientists and analysts, indexers, cataloguers and information analysts are often very skilled at summarizing data in their work. You should also develop such skills.

Textual data can be summarized in different ways. We will now explain some of the methods with the following paragraph of textual data (Table 18.1):

Table 18.1: A paragraph of textual data

A management information system (MIS) comprises the data and information processing and management activities within each organization. Such activities are responsible for collecting and storing data for an organization, as well as producing information from the data to assist managers in the planning and controlling of all organizational activities. A system is usually described in terms of its input, processing, storage and output objectives, facilities and activities. MIS is thus a system whose ultimate objective is to produce the different information required for decision-making at all levels of an organization. MIS obtains data as input from the different departments of the organization and from it's environment, and processes the data as appropriate to produce informative reports as its output. MIS also creates and maintains facilities and performs activities for storing, retrieving, and communicating data and information to managers and other personnel of the organization. The main difference between a manual organizational information system and a management information system is the use of computer and related technologies in the latter to assist how data are recorded, stored, processed, communicated and reported. (182 words)

(i) Extract important sentences:
This method entails selecting or extracting the most important data in a wholesome data to represent the data. For instance, the most informative sentences in a paragraph of sentences might be selected to represent the paragraph.

Hence, using this method, the following sentences might be extracted from Table 18.1 to represent the data in the table:

A management information system comprises the data and information processing and management activities within each organization. Such activities are responsible for collecting and storing data for an organization, as well as producing information from the data to assist managers in the planning and controlling of all organizational activities. The main difference between a manual organizational information system and a management information system is the use of computer and related technologies in the latter to assist how data are recorded, stored, processed, communicated and reported. (84 words)

This method is usually described as extracting of textual data. The above summary is also known as an extract.

(ii) Write an abstract:
This method involves writing new but fewer and shorter sentences to convey as much information as possible from the original paragraph. For example, a 10-sentence paragraph might be re-written as a two-sentence summary or abstract. Using this method, an appropriate abstract or summary of the data in Table 18.1 might look like this:

Management information system (MIS) comprises the activities in an organization that use computers and related technologies for collecting, processing and managing the data resources of the organization. MIS performs data and information input, processing, storage, retrieval, communication and output processes within the organization. (43 words)

This method is usually described as abstracting of textual data. The above summary is also known as an abstract.

(iii) Select some or all key terms or phrases
This method is also similar to methods (i) and (ii) above. It entails selecting some of the important terms or phrases in the paragraph to represent the paragraph. Examples of terms and phrases are 'management information system' and 'computer and related technologies'. Hence, using this method, the following single words might be selected from the data in Table 18.1 to describe the data:

Management information system, information processing and management, managers, planning and controlling, organizational activities, computer and related technologies. (17 words)

This method is usually described as phrase indexing of textual data. However, some people also refer to the method as key word indexing. The above terms or phrases are also known as key word index terms.

(iv) Select some or all of the key words:
This method is similar to method (1) above. It entails selecting some of the important single words in the paragraph to represent the paragraph. Nouns and long or technical words are usually regarded as important for this purpose. Hence, using this method, the following single words might be selected from the data in Table 18.1 to describe the data:

Management, information, system, processing, data input, storage, output, objectives, facilities, retrieving, communicating, managers, computer (14 words)

This method is usually described as key word indexing of textual data. The above key words are also known as key word index terms.

(v) **Coin an appropriate subject phrase or topic**
This method involves coining a subject or topic for the paragraph. Hence, using this method, the data in Table 18.1 could be described with the following subject term or phrase:

Management information systems (3 words)

This method is usually described as subject indexing of data. The above subject term or phrase is known as an subject index term.

Notice how the data (number of words) that have been used to summarize the data in Table 18.1 have reduced the data in the table from the original 182 words, through methods (i) to (v), to just three. Of course, there are differences in the effectiveness of each method for summarizing the data.

Which do you consider to be the most effective in conveying information about the original passage of text in Table 18.1?

Extracting, abstracting, key word indexing, phrase indexing, subject cataloguing, and other methods are often used in libraries, archives and record centres for summarizing data and information about the books, journals, newspapers, files and other types of documents that they acquire and stock. These information service organizations create and store extracts, abstracts, and key word and subject index terms in order to save data storage space, and so that these data summaries can later be searched to find and retrieve information about the documents.

Exercise 18.1:

Use' the four different data summarization methods of this section to summarize the information conveyed in the following passage:

Prose writing involves composing and organizing mostly textual data in the form of words, sentences, paragraphs and other language units. The subject and format of prose also range from a news story in, a newspaper, a fiction story in a story book, to a summarized report on a product marketing strategy, and to an article in a scientific journal. Writing effective prose requires a mastery of not only the grammar of a language, but also knowledge of appropriate styles of discourse in different contexts. Thus, a style that is okay for a scientific journal article would probably be too technical for a publication intended for the general public. Proposal writing, is a special case of prose writing. However, the objective of a written proposal, usually, is to sell a product or service by convincing the prospective client of the ability of the product or service to meet the client's requirements' better than any other competing product or service. The product or service might be a military tank, an information product, or expertise in designing and implementing an information system.

18.6 Analyzing structured and numeric data

You have so far learned about different methods for analyzing and summarizing textual data. However, there probably are more methods available for analyzing and summarizing structured and numerical data than there are for textual data. So let us turn our attention to structured and numerical data.

You learned in Unit 7 that structured data are data that have been subdivided into small separately meaningful subsets. Table 18.2 shows such data. Note that the structured data in the table could have been collected through a questionnaire survey or extracted from a database table. Note also that structured data could be textual (e.g. name and sex), or numeric (e.g., age and income). The question for us here is how such structured data can be summarized or analyzed.

Table 18.2: Sample structured data

Name	Sex	Age (years)	Income (Naira)
Ahmed Dogo	Male	25	12,000
Francis Eze	Male	30	35,000
Aishat Lawal	Female	51	66,500
Mary Samuel	Female	20	24,800
Ayo Gidado	Male	33	30,500
Kinsley Jeje	Male	31	15,500
Biodun Afonja	Female	18	37,200
Agnes Okoro	Female	42	26,650
Ngozi Kelechi	Female	27	34,700
Adisa Atiba	Female	33	28,300
Henry Aziza	Male	37	8,500
Funmi Cardoso	Female	19	52,000

The disciplines of mathematics and statistics have designed various methods for analyzing and summarizing structured data. Among the most common methods are (i) frequency counts, (ii) bar and pie charts, sums and averages. We will only explain these here.

Frequency counts and tables of data

The method of frequency counts of data involves counting the number of times that different specific types of data occur in some data. For example, one may count to find out how many times the different alphabetic characters (a, b, c ...) are repeated in this sentence. Do it as an exercise.

Referring to Table 18.2, you will confirm that there are seven of 'females' and five of 'males' in the column for sex. Table 18.3 shows the frequency tables that can be constructed to summarize the data in the sex and age columns of Table 18.2. Note that in the frequency table for age, the categories of age, instead of actual ages, are shown. The categories are: under 20 years, 20-29 years, 30-39 years, over 39 years. The categories are also known as classes of the data.

Table 18.3: Sample frequency tables.

Frequency table for Sex

Data value	Frequency	Percentage
Female	7	58.3
Male	5	41.6
Total	12	100

Frequency table for Age

Data category	Frequency	Percentage
Under 20 years	2	16.7
20-29 years	3	25.0
30-39 years	5	41.6
Over 39 years	2	16.7
Total	12	100

> **Exercise 18.2:**
>
> Construct frequency tables for the data in the income column of Table 18.2.

Bar and pie charts of data

Bar and pie charts are graphical ways of summarizing and analyzing data. A bar chart comprises of either shaded vertical or horizontal bars, with one bar representing a distinct data value or category. Moreover, the height or length of each bar depends on the frequency of the data type in the set of data being analyzed or summarized. Figure 18.1 (a) is a horizontal bar chart for the data in the sex column of Table 18.2. Similarly, Figure 18.1 (b) is a vertical bar chart for the data in the age column of Table 18.2.

A pie chart uses segments of a circle to represent the percentage frequency of each distinct data value or category. From high school you know that the angle of a complete circle is 360 degrees. From Table 18.3 you will also note that total percentage frequency of all data values or categories is 100. Hence, to construct a pie chart, you should convert the percentage frequency of each data value or category into the equivalent percentage of the 360 degrees.

For example, there are seven of Females' out of the 12 data values in the sex column of Table 18.3. Hence, in a circle, females will be represented by a segment of size 7/12 times 360 degrees = 210 degrees. In the same way, males will be represented by a segment of size 5/12 times 360 degrees = 150 degrees. Hence, the pie chart for the data in the sex column of Table 18.2 will be a circle divided into two segments of sizes 210 degrees and 150 degrees respectively. Figure 18.2 shows the pie charts for the data on sex and age respectively.

Sums and averages of numeric data

Two other very common methods for summarizing or analyzing numerical data is to calculate the sum or the average of the data values. Accordingly, the data in the age and income columns of Table 18.2 can be summed or averaged as required.

Exercise 18.2:

Construct bar and pie charts for the data in the income column of Table 18.2.

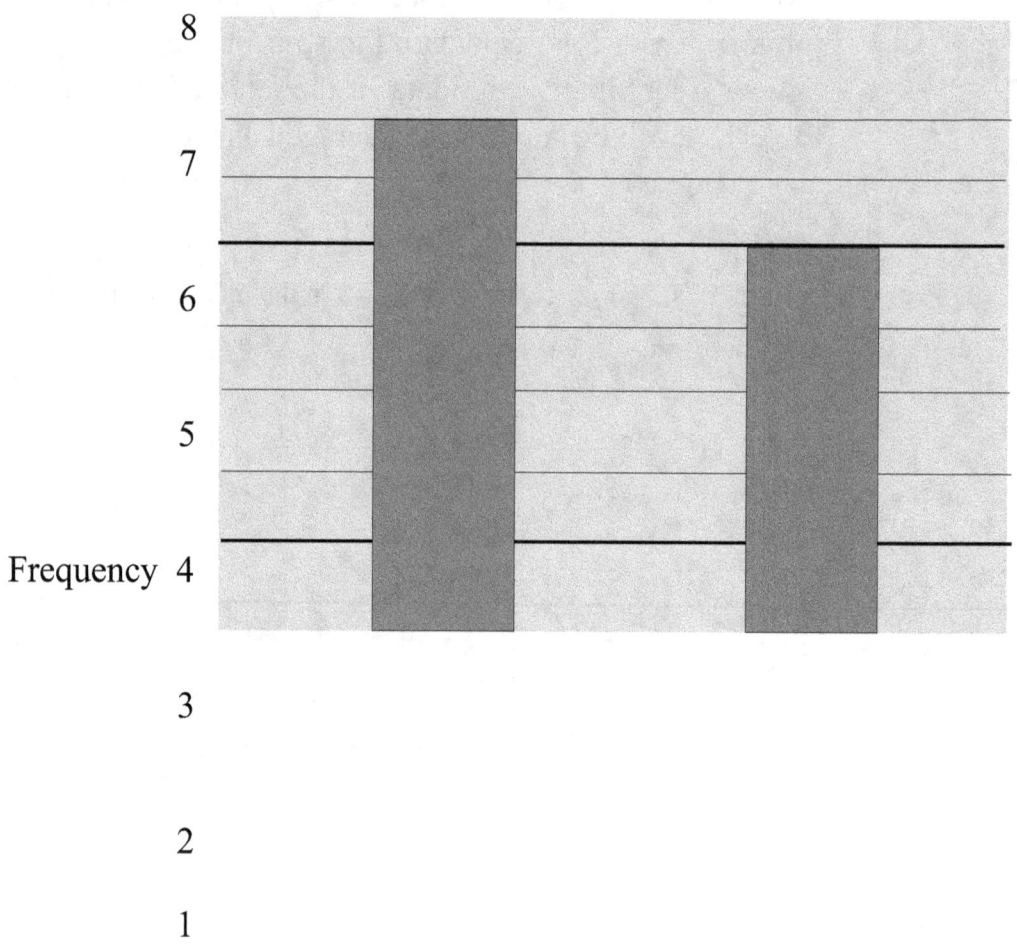

Figure 18.1(a): Bar chart of data on Sex

Figure 18.1 (b) Bar Chart of data on Age

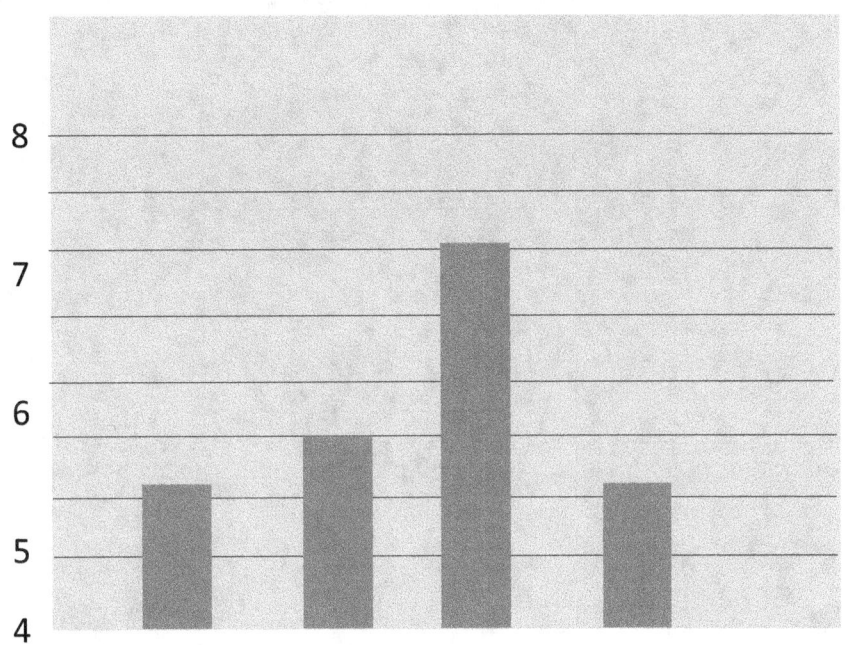

Age

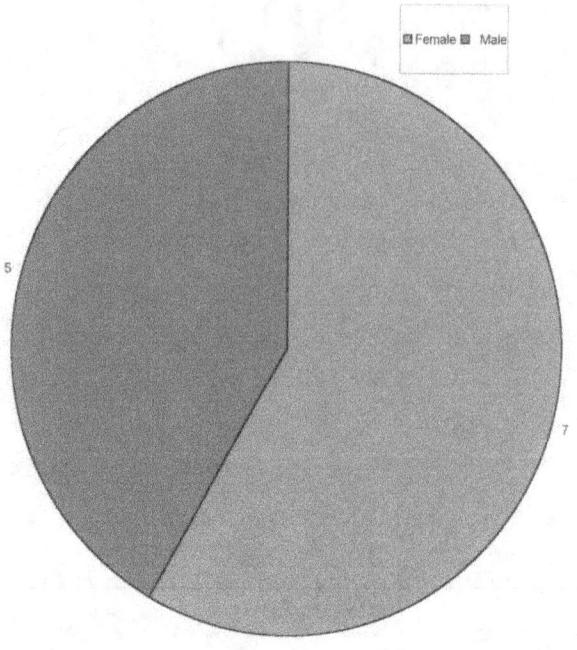

Figure 18.2(a): Pie chart of data on Sex

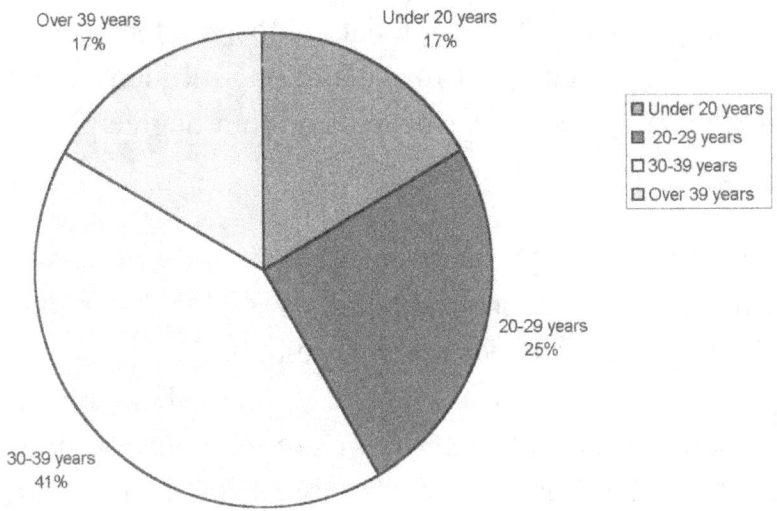

Figure 18.2(b): Pie chart of data on Age

18.7 Computerized data analyses

We have highlighted in this unit only a few of the very simple methods for analyzing and summarizing data. There are of course numerous other statistical methods and procedures for analyzing, summarizing, transforming and aggregating structured and numerical data. There are also methods for describing the relationships amongst sets of data. Most of these methods also entail the use of statistical formula. You will learn about some of the methods in the statistics courses of your degree program.

Before computers where invented data analysis was performed manually, using sheer brainwork, assisted by hand or desk calculators. However, when large volume data must be analyzed using complex statistical formula, manual methods of data analysis become tedious, error-prone, and sometimes just impossible. Nowadays, computers are used to analyze large sets of data.

Numerous computer software has been created for analyzing data. They can be categorized into two types: those designed for analyzing most kinds of structured and numeric data, and special purpose software for analyzing such data in particular disciplines such as economics, medicine, demography, etc. Software for data analysis include the Statistical Package for the Social Sciences (SPSS), Statistical Analysis System (SAS), Biomedical Programs (BMDP), Minitab, Microfit, PC-Give, Time Series Processor (TSP), EPI- INFO, etc. Some of this software have special functions and are tailored to the needs of specific groups of users. For example, TSP is often used by economists to analyze time series data. There is also software for automatic extracting, abstracting and indexing of textual data.

18.8 Conclusion

Data and information are created, analyzed and used in all disciplines and professions. Many of these disciplines have developed different methods for analyzing their data. You have learned only a few of these methods in this Unit. Data analysis and summarization are usually performed during data interpretation and use, and sometimes before data are stored. Hence, data analysis and summarization are an important data management activity.

18.9 Summary

In this unit, you have learned about data analysis and summarization as an important data management activity.

Data analysis is the process of investigating and identifying the attributes or characteristics of a particular set of data. Data analysis usually entails data summarization, transformation, aggregation and disaggregation. Data summarization is the process of reducing some voluminous data into less voluminous data. Data transformation is the process of converting one type of data into another. Data aggregation refers to the process of merging two or more originally separate sets of data into a single set of data, whereas data disaggregation refers to the process of breaking or decomposing some data into two or more separate data sets. Data may be aggregated during or after collection.

Data summarization is often performed with textual data which often tend to be voluminous. For instance, the data in a whole book, or in a chapter of the book, or in a paragraph of a chapter, could be summarized into less voluminous textual data such as a single sentence, or a subject phrase.

Textual data can be summarized in different ways, among which are: (i) extraction of important sentences; (ii) writing of an abstract; (iii) selecting key terms or phrases selecting key words, and (v) coining a subject phrase or topic. Various methods have also been designed for analyzing and summarizing structured data. Among the most basic methods are (i) frequency counts, (ii) bar and pie charts, and (iii) sums and averages, of data. Numerous computer software have also been created for analyzing data. They can be categorized into two types: those designed for analyzing most kinds of structured and numeric data, and special purpose software for analyzing textual and numeric data in particular disciplines.

18.10 Self-assessment exercises

1. Which of extracting, abstracting, key word indexing, and subject cataloguing methods of summarizing textual data do you consider the best, and why?

2. Write out (a) a short extract, (b) a short abstract, and (c) a key word index for the introduction of this unit.
3. Construct (a) a frequency table, and (b) a bar chart, for the following set of numbers:

    20, 34, 42, 56, 66, 47, 55, 67, 40, 52, 53, 70, 83, 23, 39, 45, 50, 69, 75, 55

    28, 33, 49, 51, 60, 79, 35, 42, 59, 65, 31, 44, 55, 62, 48, 52, 11, 15, 45, 58

18.11 References

S.O. Adamu and T.L Johnson Statistics for Beginners BK 1. Ibadan: Evans Brothers NG (Publishers) Ltd. 1985.

DESIGNING AND IMPLEMENTING INFORMATION SYSTEMS FOR DATA MANAGEMENT

Table of Contents	
19.1	Introduction
19.2	Objectives
19.3	Data management revisited
19.4	Information systems revisited
19.5	The process of designing systems for data management
(1)	Ascertaining users' information requirements
(2)	Feasibility study of candidate new systems
(3)	Detailed analysis of old system
(4)	Designing the new system
(5)	Implementing the new system
(6)	Operating the new system
(7)	Periodic evaluation of the new system
19.6	Conclusion
19.7	Summary

19.1 Introduction

So far in this course we have discussed how data and information are managed in different contexts and information systems to produce information for people. However, no matter how well designed initially, data and information management systems eventually become obsolete. An obsolete system is a system whose information output is no longer needed, or whose data management activities (input, process, storage, communication, and output) are outmoded or no longer cost-effective. A major cause of system obsolescence is change - changes in nature, changes in human behavior, and in mankind's knowledge about nature and society. For instance, people across all parts of the world are becoming more and more literate, educated, and information conscious. Hence, a leading-edge information system today is likely to become outmoded tomorrow. Moreover, scientific studies of nature and human behavior are not only producing new technologies, but also providing new insights into how to design data and information management activities and systems.

A data and information management system are deemed ripe for improvement or replacement when it becomes unable to provide adequate information for the people for which it was designed. This raises the important issue of how to go about improving or replacing such an obsolete system.

In this unit you will learn about some standard procedures for designing a new information system to replace an existing, but obsolete one.

19.2 Objectives

After studying this unit, you should be able to:

1. Describe the stages of activities for developing new information systems.
2. Explain the importance of periodic assessment of the information and data requirements of the users of an information system.
3. Explain the importance of periodic evaluation of the data and information management performance of an information system.

19.3 Data management revisited

Figure 19.1 shows the data management cycle of activities that was first introduced in Unit 2. You will also recall from Unit 3 that data management activities are usually performed within information systems that have been designed for the purpose.

Figure 19.1
The data (information) life-cycle of activities

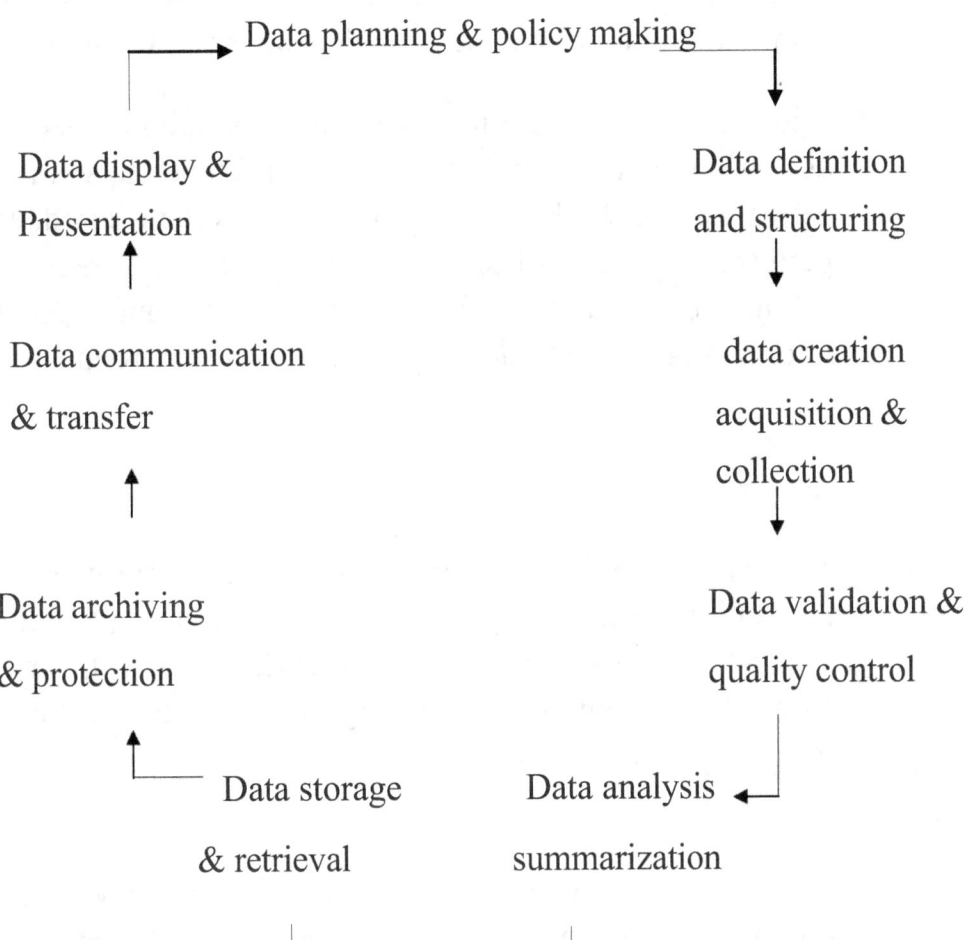

An information system is designed to provide data or information to different categories of people. Examples of such categories of people are the managers or lower-level employees of an organization, customers of a business firm, citizens in a community, library patrons, people who surf the Internet, etc.

With reference to Figure 19.1, an information system may be designed to perform all of the different data management activities. Usually however, information systems are developed to perform only some of the activities. However, such systems must obtain their data input from other systems, and/or supply their information output to other systems in their environment.

19.4 Information systems revisited

You will also recall from Unit 3 that information systems invariably have sub-systems. Hence, even if an information system is designed to perform all the data management activities, each of the activities may be assigned to a different sub-system of the information system.

All the sub-systems of an information system may be developed, improved or replaced at the same time. But different sub-systems of an information system can also be, and are sometimes, developed at different times. However, irrespective of when and how frequently a sub-system is developed or improved, it must always be designed to work in harmony with the other sub-systems of the information system.

Information systems and sub-systems also require resources for performing their data management activities, as was explained in Unit 3. Among such resources are people to perform various roles and activities, physical space, equipment, organizational systems, energy and time.

Exercise 19.1

Based on the knowledge about information systems that you have so far gained in this course, describe the input, storage, process and output activities of a system designed to only validate and control the quality of collected data.

19.5 The process of designing systems for data management

Information systems are best designed and developed through a systematic planning process. Otherwise, the whole process can get out of hand and fail.

As already explained, data management functions are usually performed by information systems designed for the purpose. In other words, the data management activities of an information system are usually planned and designed when the system itself is being planned or designed.

The process of planning or designing an information system is often referred to as the information system development life cycle (SDLC) or system development cycle (SDC). The system development cycle, much like the data management cycle of activities, are sequences of activities that are often performed in order to develop a new information system or to improve an existing one.

The system development cycle comprises of the following seven stages of activities:

(1) Ascertaining users' information requirements
(2) Feasibility study of candidate new systems
(3) Detailed analysis of the old system
(4) Designing the new system
(5) Implementing of the new system
(6) Operating of new system
(7) Monitoring and evaluating the new system

We will explain each of the above stages of activities in the remaining sections of this Unit. You should keep in mind that the stages are sequential in the sense that a system designer is expected to begin with stage (1) and end with stage (7). However, designers of information systems and sub-systems often back track and repeat the first few stages in order to ensure that a designed system will provide the data and information required by the people when it is established and operated. Moreover, a stage (7) of a system development cycle often leads to the stage (1) of a subsequent cycle.

(1) Ascertaining users' information requirements

This is usually the first stage of the system development life cycle. As explained above, information systems are invariably established to provide information for information system for such people (often referred to as information users) by finding out what types of data and information they will want to have.

The objective of this stage of activities is, firstly, to determine the category of people for which the new information system will provide information. A second objective is to determine the kinds and forms of information and data that the users will require from the system.

Hence, studies are undertaken during this stage to find out the types of data or information that users will require either in order to do their work, to improve their education, or to live well. The studies are usually in the form of surveys of users and the way they work, study or live through questionnaires or forms, and or by directly observing the users at work, home or school as the case may be. In other words, data and information will be collected and analyzed to determine the types of information that the new system should provide for potential system users.

(2) Feasibility study of candidate new systems

Once the information requirements of users are determined, other studies are undertaken to find out whether it will be possible (i.e., feasible) to design and establish a new system to acquire and process data for producing the information required by the users. Feasibility studies aim to find out whether resources will be available to design, establish and operate the proposed new information system. Among the required resources are:

- Money to acquire other resources;
- Skilled people to operate the system;
- Equipment, such as computers for capturing, processing, storing and
- producing data and information;
- Appropriate physical space for the system;
- Electrical energy to operate the equipment of the system;
- Organization system, such as new organizational units, to provide a management and environment for the new system;
- Time to plan and implement the system; etc.

In other words, feasibility studies are done to find out if money will be available as and when needed to finance the establishment of the new system; whether the computer and other equipment and physical space required by the new system can be acquired; whether the required human resources can be can be hired and trained to operate the proposed system; whether such public services as electricity and telephone that the new system might require are available, and if not, whether alternatives can be provided, etc.

(3) Detailed analysis of old system

This is a stage for yet another set of studies. The stage involves in- depth studies of the existing information system that is now to be improved or replaced by the new one. The old system may be a manual system, in which no computers are used at all. Or it may be an old and obsolete computerized system. There also might not be an existing system, in which case studies will be undertaken on information systems for similar users in other places.

The in-depth study of the old system usually aim to find out how data are being managed by the old system: that is, what policies, procedures, equipment, human resources, etc., are being used by the old system for various data management activities? The studies also aim to find out ineffective aspects of old system that should be improved, as well as good aspects of the old system that should be carried over to the proposed new system.

Aspects of the old system that are studied include:

- The types of data and information are being created, acquired, stored, processed, communicated and produced in the old system;
- The volume and frequency with which data and information are being created, acquired, stored, processed, communicated and produced in the old system;
- The types of equipment (typewriters, calculators, computers, peripherals, telephones, photocopiers, etc) that are being used in the old system;
- the types, number, qualifications and skills of the people who are working in the old system; the departments, committees, and other administrative units that are responsible for supervising the different data management activities in the old system;
- The procedural steps that are being used for performing each of the data management activities in the old system;
- The policies that are being followed in performing different data management activities in the old system;
- The problems being encountered by users of the old system;

Studies of the existing system aim to collect data and information for improving the system designer's knowledge about the existing system. With that knowledge, the designer will then be better placed to determine the best way to design the new system. Of course, the new system should improve the good aspects of the old system, as well as avoid the bad aspects of the old system

Exercise 19.2

Assume that a friend of yours who presently has no computer system in his/her home desires to have one installed. List all the constraints that are likely to jeopardize the feasibility of such a plan.

(4) Designing the new system

Just as an architect carefully designs a building before it is actually built, the information system designer must design the features of the new system during this stage. The system designer is expected to describe in as much detail as possible how the new system will look like. The description is usually very detailed covering many different aspects of the new system, including (pay attention to the italicized words):

- The *information users* for which the new system is planned;
- *Types and nature of information* to be provided by the new system when established;
- The types of *reports* containing information to be printed or displayed on computer screens by the system;
- The types and nature of *data* to be created, acquired or collected for producing information and other data;
- The types of *data collection forms* that should be designed for collecting data for input into the databases of the system;
- The types of *databases* that should be created for storing data in the system, and the type of computer media that should be used for storing the database;
- The types of *data management activities* to be performed on the data, including data validation, storage and retrieval, analysis, transfer, etc;
- The different smaller *tasks* to be performed in each data management activity;
- The different *classes and number of personnel* (data clerks, supervisors, managers, etc) required to perform the activities and tasks;
- The types of *training* that existing employees should undergo to operate and manage the system; the types of

training that the envisaged information end users of the system should undergo;
- The different types and number of equipment (computers, modems, telephone lines, to be installed and used by the system;
- The type of communication connections that should be used to link up the different equipment to form a telephone or computer networks;
- The types of computer software that should be installed in the computer hardware to facilitate the various data processing activities.
- The types of committees, departments and units that should be created to supervise the system;
- The types of publicity and enlightenment campaigns that should be mounted to persuade all potential users and operators of the system to accept the system.
- The types of system tests that should be performed before the system is commissioned for use, as well as the procedures to be followed in changing over fully from the old to the new system. etc.

Of course, by the time the system designer describes all the above and other aspects of the proposed new system, it will be clear what system is being planned. The designer's description is invariably provided in a report known as the system blueprint. It is the blueprint that is expected to be carefully followed during the actual implementation of the new system.

(5) Implementing the new system

This is the stage when the blueprint of the new system is implemented by system implementers. However, a system designer might implement his own blueprint. System implementation is likely to encounter less problems if the system design is very good, and the blueprint is well written.

It is very important that the implementation of the new system is considered and executed as a project in its own right. This is the stage when most of the money required for establishing the system will actually be spent - on equipment, software, databases, hiring and training new personnel, etc. Hence, adequate care in implementing the new system is required.

In order for you to appreciate the importance of the system implementation stage, you need to know a few things about projects and their implementation.

A project is defined as a set of interconnected activities that begin at a specific date and end at another specific date. That is, a project must have definite timing and duration. A project also requires adequate resources for its implementation. The number of resources required for a project also depends on the timing and duration of the project implementation. Delays in project implementation often led to increases in the cost of project implementation. Hence, there is the need to implement a project within time, so that its costs can be kept within limits.

The implementation of a project to establish a new information system entail performing various activities toward establishing the system as described in the system blueprint. To do proper job of this, system implementers should:

- Define the different tasks to be performed during project implementation (e.g. publicize the system, train personnel, acquire and install hardware, acquire and install software, create databases, etc).

- Estimate adequate time for doing the different tasks. Some tasks can often be performed simultaneously, so that time savings can be made. Note also that time can sometimes be bought with money, for instance, by hiring four persons instead of two persons to perform a task.

- Estimate the quantities of the other resources needed for doing the different tasks, such as money, human resources, etc.,

  Prepare a budget of how much money all the tasks will cost.

- Negotiate and make sure that money and other resources will be available as and when needed to perform all tasks so that project implementation will not be delayed.

- Establish a project implementation organization (committee, project manager, technical staff, support staff, etc) to oversee the project implementation process.

- Flag off the project implementation process, and make a success of it by following the blueprint created by the system designer, as well as the project implementation plans.

Effective project implementation invariably demands good project management skills and adequate resources.

> **Exercise 19.3**
>
> Describe in detail the various activities you will perform in order to ensure that you acquire the most appropriate computer system for your friend from Exercise 20.2.

(6) Operating the new system

This stage begins only when the system has been completely established and tested. That is, when people have been trained, when equipment and software have been installed, when a database has been created, when forms for collecting data have been printed, when organizational departments or units to oversee the system have been established, when users have been informed and trained, etc.

Operating the new information system involves using the new system for performing the different data management tasks for which the system was established. In other words, operating the new system entails running the system to provide valuable information for its users. Operating the system also entail making sure that the system keeps operating smoothly for as long as possible, or until a new system is designed and established to replace it. To do this, the system must be continuously provided with operating resources. The system should also be continuously monitored and maintained.

(7) Periodic evaluation of the new system

All information systems should be evaluated periodically to find out whether they are working well. They should be evaluated to ascertain whether they are continuing to perform appropriate data management activities to produce information for its users.

The best information system for a class of users today will eventually become obsolete tomorrow. There can be many reasons for this:

- Most of the users may, over time, be replaced by others. New users may have different information requirements;
- Better types of data for producing the information may become available, but the old system cannot handle them well;
- Better procedures for performing the various data management activities may be invented. This may put the old system at a disadvantage compared to other systems;
- Better equipment for capturing, storing, communicating, processing data may become available; etc.

As noted earlier, an information system is deemed obsolete if it is no longer able to provide adequate information for its users, or that it has become too costly to maintain and operate. For example, it may be impossible to find replacement parts for some of the old equipment. When a system is deemed obsolete a process should be started to replace it with a new system. This flags of the start off a new system development cycle of activities.

19.6 Conclusion

All new information should be implemented by following a planned process. The system development cycle of activities is one such process. In other words, a new information system is likely to fail if it is not planned carefully. This requires that the first four stages of activities in the system development cycle are performed well by experienced people. However, a well planned new information system can also fail if it is not carefully implemented. This requires that the implementation of the project is considered as a project that must be completed during a definite period. Finally, even if an information system project is implemented well, it may still fail if it is not consistently operated, monitored and maintained.

19.7 Summary

In this unit, you have learned about the system development life cycle of activities. This is one of the well-known standard processes often used for developing new information systems. The cycle of activities comprises the following: study of users' information requirements; feasibility study of candidate new systems; detailed study of the old system; design of the new system; implementation of the new system; operation of the new system; and monitoring and evaluating the new system. The last activity, ie, monitoring and evaluating the new system, sometimes lead to the start of a new cycle of activities, particularly when a system becomes obsolete. An obsolete information system is a system whose information output is no longer needed, or whose data management activities are outmoded or no longer cost-effective. A new system stands a good chance of success if it is well planned, implemented and operated. On the other hand, unplanned or poorly planned and implemented information systems usually fail.